Step by Step Azure Site Recovery

With Different ASR Scenarios

Chetan Pawar

Bachelor's in Computers (**B.E.**)
MCSA, MCSA, MCTS, MCITP
Windows 2000, 2003, 2008, 2012, Exchange 2003, 2007, 2010, 2013
Windows XP, 7 and 8 Clients, VMware, Hyper-V and Cloud Computing
CompTIA, HP and Dell Certified Technician
Microsoft Certified Trainer (**MCT**) since August 2004

ISBN-13: 978-1519434500

ISBN-10:1519434502

Table of Contents

This step by step book is aimed as a guide to deploy Site Recovery to:

- **Protect VMware virtual machines**—Coordinate replication, failover, and recovery of on-premises VMware virtual machines to Azure

- **Protect physical servers**—Coordinate replication, failover, and recovery of on-premises physical Windows and Linux servers to Azure using the Azure Site Recovery service.

The workbook includes an overview, deployment prerequisites, and set up instructions to set up Azure ASR. At the end we have also put together various scenarios in which Azure ASR can be put together as a state-of-the-art Automated Site Recovery Solution.

What is Azure Site Recovery?

The Azure Site Recovery contributes to your business continuity and disaster recovery (BCDR) strategy by orchestrating replication, failover and recovery of virtual machines and physical servers. Machines can be replicated to Azure, or to a secondary on-premises data center.

How does it protect on-premises resources?

Site Recovery helps protect your on-premises resources by orchestrating, simplifying replication, failover and failback in a number of **deployment scenarios**. If you want to protect your on-premises VMware virtual machines or Windows or Linux physical servers here's how Site Recovery can help:

- Allows VMware users to replicate virtual machines to Azure.

- Allows the replication of physical on-premises servers to Azure.

- Provides a single location to setup and manage replication, failover, and recovery.

- Provides easy failover from your on-premises infrastructure to Azure, and failback (restore) from Azure to on-premises.

- Implements recovery plans for easy failover of workloads that are tiered over multiple machines.

- Provides multi VM consistency so that virtual machines and physical servers running specific workloads can be recovered together to a consistent data point.

- Supports data replication over the Internet, over a site-to-site VPN connection, or over Azure ExpressRoute.

- Provides automated discovery of VMware virtual machines.

What do I need?

This diagram shows the deployment components.

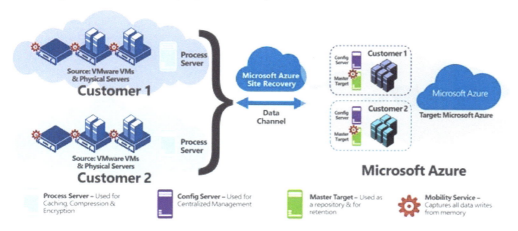

Here's what you'll need:

COMPONENT	DEPLOYMENT	DETAILS
Configuration server	Deploy as a Azure standard A3 virtual machine in the same subscription as Site Recovery. You set up in the Site Recovery portal	This server coordinates communication between protected machines, the process server, and master target servers in Azure. It sets up replication and coordinates recovery in Azure when failover occurs.
Master target Server	Deploy as Azure virtual machine — Either a Windows server based on a Windows Server 2012 R2 gallery image (to protect Windows machines) or as a Linux server based on a OpenLogic CentOS 6.6 gallery image (to protect Linux machines). Three sizing options are available – Standard A4, Standard D14 and Standard DS4. The server is connected to the same Azure network as the configuration server. You set up in the Site Recovery portal	It receives and retains replicated data from your protected machines using attached VHDs created on blob storage in your Azure storage account. Select Standard DS4 specifically for configuring protection for workloads requiring consistent high performance and low latency using Premium Storage Account.
Process server	Deploy as an on-premises virtual or physical server running	Protected machines send replication data to the on-

COMPONENT	DEPLOYMENT	DETAILS
	Windows Server 2012 R2 We recommend it's placed on the same network and LAN segment as the machines that you want to protect, but it can run on a different network as long as protected machines have L3 network visibility to it. You set it up and register it to the configuration server in the Site Recovery portal.	premises process server. It has a disk-based cache to cache replication data that it receives. It performs a number of actions on that data. It optimizes data by caching, compressing, and encrypting it before sending it on to the master target server. It handles push installation of the Mobility Service. It performs automatic discovery of VMware virtual machines.
On-premises machines	On-premises virtual machines running on a VMware hypervisor, or physical servers running Windows or Linux.	You set up replication settings that apply to virtual machines and servers. You can fail over an individual machine or more commonly, as part of a recovery plan containing multiple virtual machines that fail over together.
Mobility service	Installs on each virtual machine or physical server you want to protect	The Mobility service send data to the Process Server as part of initial replication (resync.) Once the server

COMPONENT	DEPLOYMENT	DETAILS
	Can be installed manually or pushed and installed automatically by the process server when protection is enabled for the server	reaches a protected state (after resync is completed) the Mobility service performs an in-memory capture of writes to disk and sends it to the Process Server. Application consistency for Windows servers is achieved using the VSS framework.
Azure Site Recovery vault	Set up after you've subscribed to the Site Recovery service.	You register servers in a Site Recovery vault. The vault coordinates and orchestrates data replication, failover, and recovery between your on-premises site and Azure.
Replication mechanism	**Over the Internet**— Communicates and replicates data from protected on-premises servers and Azure using a secure SSL/TLS communication channel over a public internet connection. This is the default option. **VPN/ExpressRoute**— Communicates and replicates data between on-premises servers and Azure over a VPN connection. You'll need to set up a site-to-site VPN or an ExpressRoute connection between	Neither option requires you to open any inbound network ports on protected machines. All network communication is initiated from the on-premises site.

COMPONENT	DEPLOYMENT	DETAILS
		the on-premises site and your Azure network.
		You'll select how you want to replicate during Site Recovery deployment. You can't change the mechanism after it's configured without impacting protection on already protected servers.

Capacity planning

Main areas for considerations are:

• **Source environment**—The VMware infrastructure, source machine settings and requirements.

• **Component servers**—The process server, configuration server, and master target server

Hyper-V protection lifecycle

This workflow shows the process for protecting, replicating, and failing over Hyper-V virtual machines.

1. **Enable protection**: You set up the Site Recovery vault, configure replication settings for a VMM cloud or Hyper-V site, and enable protection for VMs. A job called **Enable Protection** is initiated and can be monitored in the **Jobs** tab. The job checks that the machine complies with prerequisites and then invokes the CreateReplicationRelationship method which sets up replication to Azure with the settings you've configured. The **Enable protection** job also invokes the StartReplication method to initialize a full VM replication.

2. **Initial replication**: A virtual machine snapshot is taken and virtual hard disks are replicated one by one until they're all copied to Azure or to the secondary datacenter. This The time to complete this depends on the size and network bandwidth and the initial replication method you've chosen. If disk changes occur while initial replication is in progress the Hyper-V Replica Replication

Tracker tracks those changes as Hyper-V Replication Logs (.hrl) that are located in the same folder as the disks. Each disk has an associated .hrl file that will be sent to secondary storage. Note that the snapshot and log files consume disk resources while initial replication is in progress. When the initial replication finishes the VM snapshot is deleted and the delta disk changes in the log are synchronized and merged.

3. **Finalize protection**: After initial replication finishes the **Finalize protection** job configures network and other post-replication settings and the virtual machine is protected. If you're replicating to Azure you might need to tweak the settings for the virtual machine so that it's ready for failover. At this point you can run a test failover to check everything's working as expected.

4. **Replication**: After initial replication delta synchronized occurs, in accordance with the replication settings and method.

- **Replication failure**: If delta replication fails and a full replication would be costly in terms of bandwidth or time then resynchronization occurs. For example if the .hrl files reach 50% of the disk size then the virtual machine will be marked for resynchronization. Resynchronization minimizes the amount of data sent by computing checksums of the source and target virtual machines and sending only the delta. After resynchronization finishes delta replication should resume. By default resynchronization is scheduled to run automatically outside office hours, but you can resynchronize a virtual machine manually.

- **Replication error**: If a replication error occurs there's a built-in retry. If it's a non-recoverable error such as an authentication or authorization error, or a replica machine in an invalid state no retry will be attempted. If it's a recoverable error such as a network error, or low disk space/memory then a retry occurs with increasing intervals between retries (1, 2, 4, 8, 10, and then every 30 minutes).

5. **Planned/unplanned failovers**: You run planned/unplanned failovers when the need arises. If you run a planned failover source VMs are shut down to ensure no data loss. After replica VMs are created they're in a commit pending state. You need to commit them to complete the failover unless you're replicating with SAN in which case commit is automatic. After the primary site is up and running failback can occur. If you've replicated to Azure reverse replication is automatic. Otherwise you kick off a reverse replication.

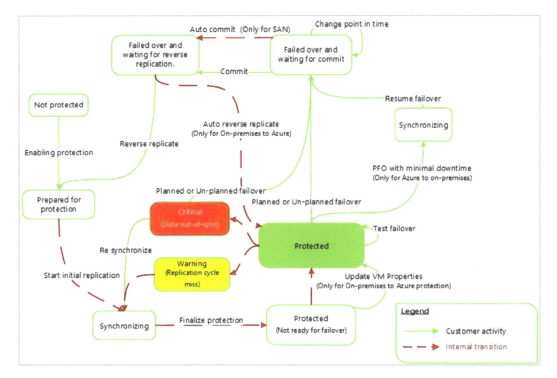

Considerations for the source environment

- **Maximum disk size**—The current maximum size of the disk that can be attached to a virtual machine is 1 TB. Thus the maximum size of a source disk that can be replicated is also limited to 1 TB.

- **Maximum size per source**—The maximum size of a single source machine is 31 TB (with 31 disks) and with a D14 instance provisioned for the master target server.

- **Number of sources per master target server**—Multiple source machines can be protected with a single master target server. However, a single source machine can't be protected across multiple master target servers, because as disks replicate, a VHD that mirrors the size of the disk is created on Azure blob storage and attached as a data disk to the master target server.

- **Maximum daily change rate per source**—There are three factors that need to be considered when considering the recommended change rate per source. For the target based considerations two IOPS are required on the target disk for each operation on the source. This is because a read of old data and a write of the new data will happen on the target disk.

- **Daily change rate supported by the process server**—A source machine can't span multiple process servers. A single process server can support up to 1 TB of daily change rate. Hence 1 TB is the maximum daily data change rate supported for a source machine.

- **Maximum throughput supported by the target disk**—Maximum churn per source disk can't be more than 144 GB/day (with 8K write size). See the table in the master target section for the throughput and IOPs of the target for various write sizes. This number must be divided by two because each source IOP generates 2 IOPS on the target disk. Refer Scalability and Performance Targets when using Premium Storage while configuring target for Premium Storage account.

- **Maximum throughput supported by the storage account**—A source can't span multiple storage accounts. Given that a storage account takes a maximum of 20,000 requests per second and that each source IOP generates 2 IOPS at the master target server, we recommend you keep the number of IOPS across the source to 10,000. Refer Scalability and Performance Targets when using Premium Storage while configuring source for Premium Storage account.

Considerations for component servers

Table 1 summarizes the virtual machine sizes for the configuration and master target servers.

COMPONENT	DEPLOYED AZURE INSTANCES	CORES	MEMORY	MAX DISKS	DISK SIZE
Configuration server	Standard A3	4	7 GB	8	1023 GB
Master target server	Standard A4	8	14 GB	16	1023 GB
	Standard D14	16	112 GB	32	1023 GB
	Standard DS4	8	28 GB	16	1023

COMPONENT	DEPLOYED AZURE INSTANCES	CORES	MEMORY	MAX DISKS	DISK SIZE
					GB

Table 1

Process server considerations

Generally process server sizing depends on the daily change rate across all protected workloads. Primary considerations include:

- You need sufficient compute to perform tasks such as inline compression and encryption.

- Process server uses disk based cache. Make sure the recommended cache space and disk throughput is available to facilitate the data changes stored in the event of network bottleneck or outage.

- Ensure sufficient bandwidth so that the process server can upload the data to the master target server to provide continuous data protection.

Table 2 provides a summary of the process server guidelines.

DATA CHANGE RATE	CPU	MEMORY	CACHE DISK SIZE	CACHE DISK THROUGHPUT	BANDWIDTH INGRESS/EGRESS
< 300 GB	4 vCPUs (2 sockets * 2 cores @ 2.5GHz)	4 GB	600 GB	7 to 10 MB per second	30 Mbps/21 Mbps

DATA CHANGE RATE	CPU	MEMORY	CACHE DISK SIZE	CACHE DISK THROUGHPUT	BANDWIDTH INGRESS/EGRESS
300 to 600 GB	8 vCPUs (2 sockets * 4 cores @ 2.5GHz)	6 GB	600 GB	11 to 15 MB per second	60 Mbps/42 Mbps
600 GB to 1 TB	12 vCPUs (2 sockets * 6 cores @ 2.5GHz)	8 GB	600 GB	16 to 20 MB per second	100 Mbps/70 Mbps
> 1 TB	Deploy another process server				

Table 2

Where:

- Ingress is download bandwidth (intranet between the source and process server).

- Egress is upload bandwidth (internet between the process server and master target server). Egress numbers presume average 30% process server compression.

- For cache disk a separate OS disk of minimum 128 GB is recommended for all process servers.

- For cache disk throughput the following storage was used for benchmarking: 8 SAS drives of 10 K RPM with RAID 10 configuration.

Configuration server considerations

Each configuration server can support up to 100 source machines with 3-4 volumes. If these numbers are exceeded we recommend you deploy another configuration server. See Table 1 for the default virtual machine properties of the configuration server.

Master target server and storage account considerations

The storage for each master target server is comprised of an OS disk, a retention volume, and data disks. The retention drive maintains the journal of disk changes for the duration of the retention window defined in the Site Recovery portal. Refer to Table 1 for the virtual machine properties of the master target server. Table 3 shows how the disks of A4 are used.

INSTANCE	OS DISK	RETENTION	DATA DISKS
		Retention	Data disks
Standard A4	1 disk (1 * 1023 GB)	1 disk (1 * 1023 GB)	15 disks (15 * 1023 GB)
Standard D14	1 disk (1 * 1023 GB)	1 disk (1 * 1023 GB)	31 disks (15 * 1023 GB)
Standard DS4	1 disk (1 * 1023 GB)	1 disk (1 * 1023 GB)	15 disks (15 * 1023 GB)

Table 3

- Capacity planning for the master target server depends on:

- Azure storage performance and limitations

- The maximum number of highly utilized disks for a Standard Tier VM, is about 40 (20,000/500 IOPS per disk) in a single storage account. Refer Scalability for more information. Similarly refer Scalability Targets for Premium Storage Accounts for more information about Premium Storage account.

- Daily change rate

- Retention volume storage.

Note that:

- One source can't span multiple storage accounts. This applies to the data disk that go to the storage accounts selected when you configure protection. The OS and the retention disks usually go to the automatically deployed storage account.

- The retention storage volume required depends on the daily change rate and the number of retention days. The retention storage required per master target server = total churn from source per day * number of retention days.

- Each master target server has only one retention volume. The retention volume is shared across the disks attached to the master target server. For example:

- If there's a source machine with 5 disks and each disk generates 120 IOPS (8K size) on the source, this translates to 240 IOPS per disk (2 operations on the target disk per source IO). 240 IOPS is within the Azure per disk IOPS limit of 500.

- On the retention volume, this becomes 120 * 5 = 600 IOPS and this can become a bottle neck. In this scenario, a good strategy would be to add more disks to the retention volume and span it across, as a RAID stripe configuration. This will improve performance because the IOPS are distributed across multiple drives. The number of drives to be added to the retention volume will be as follows:

- Total IOPS from source environment / 500

- Total churn per day from source environment (uncompressed) / 287 GB. 287 GB is the maximum throughput supported by a target disk per day. This metric will vary based on the write size with a factor of 8K, because in this case 8K is thee assumed write size. For example, if the write size is 4K then throughput will be 287/2. And if the write size is 16K then throughput will be 287*2.
- The number of storage accounts required = total source IOPs/10000.

Before you start

COMPONENT	REQUIREMENTS	DETAILS
Azure account	You'll need a Microsoft Azure account. You can start with a free trial.	
Azure storage	You'll need an Azure storage account to store replicated data Either the account should be a Standard Geo-redundant Storage Account or Premium Storage Account. It must in the same region as the Azure Site Recovery service, and be associated with the same subscription. To learn more read Introduction to Microsoft Azure Storage	
Azure virtual network	You'll need an Azure virtual network on which the configuration server and master target server will be deployed. It should be in the same subscription and region as the Azure Site Recovery vault. If you wish to replicate data over an ExpressRoute or VPN connection the Azure virtual network must be connected to your on-premises network over an ExpressRoute connection or a Site-to-Site VPN.	
Azure resources	Make sure you have enough Azure resources to deploy all components. Read more in Azure Subscription Limits.	
Azure virtual	Virtual machines you want to protect should	

COMPONENT	REQUIREMENTS	DETAILS
machines	conform with Azure prerequisites. **Disk count**—A maximum of 31 disks can be supported on a single protected server **Disk sizes**—Individual disk capacity shouldn't be more than 1023 GB **Clustering**—Clustered servers aren't supported **Boot**—Un fied Extensible Firmware Interface(UEFI)/Extensible Firmware Interface(EFI) boot isn't supported **Volumes**—Bit locker encrypted volumes aren't supported **Server names**—Names should contain between 1 and 63 characters (letters, numbers and hyphens). The name must start with a letter or number and end with a letter or number. After a machine is protected you can modify the Azure name.	
Configuration server	Standard A3 virtual machine based on an Azure Site Recovery Windows Server 2012 R2 gallery image will be created in your subscription for the configuration server. It's created as the first instance in a new cloud service. If you select Public Internet as the connectivity type for the Configuration Server the cloud service will be created with a reserved public IP address. The installation path should be in English characters only.	

COMPONENT	REQUIREMENTS	DETAILS
Master target server	Azure virtual machine, standard A4, D14 or DS4. The installation path should be in English characters only. For example the path should be **/usr/local/ASR** for a master target server running Linux.	
Process server	You can deploy the process server on physical or virtual machine running Windows Server 2012 R2 with the latest updates. Install on C:/. We recommend you place the server on the same network and subnet as the machines you want to protect. Install VMware vSphere CLI 5.5.0 on the process server. The VMware vSphere CLI component is required on the process server in order to discover virtual machines managed by a vCenter server or virtual machines running on an ESXi host. The installation path should be in English characters only. ReFS File System is not supported.	
VMware	A VMware vCenter server managing your VMware vSphere hypervisors. It should be running vCenter version 5.1 or 5.5 with the latest updates. One or more vSphere hypervisors containing VMware virtual machines you want to protect. The hypervisor should be running ESX/ESXi version 5.1	

COMPONENT	REQUIREMENTS	DETAILS
	or 5.5 with the latest updates.	
	VMware virtual machines should have VMware tools instal ed and running.	
Windows machines	Protected physical servers or VMware virtual machines running Windows have a number of requirements.	
	A supported 64-bit operating system: **Windows Server 2012 R2**, **Windows Server 2012**, or **Windows Server 2008 R2 with at least SP1**.	
	The host name, mount points, device names, Windows system path (eg: C:\Windows) should be in English only.	
	The operating system should be installed on C:\ drive.	
	Only basic disks are supported. Dynamic disks aren't supported.	
	You'll need to provide an administrator account (must be a local administrator on the Windows machine) to push install the Mobility Service on Windows servers. If the provided account is a non-domain account you'll need to disable Remote User Access control on the local machine. To do this add the LocalAccountTokenFilterPolicy DWORD registry entry with a value of 1 under HKEY_LOCAL_MACHINE\SOFTWARE\Microsoft\Windows\CurrentVersion\Policies\System. To add the registry entry from a CLI open cmd or powershell	

COMPONENT	REQUIREMENTS	DETAILS
	and enter `REG ADD HKEY_LOCAL_MACHINE\SOFTWARE\Microsoft\Windows\CurrentVersion\Policies\System /v LocalAccountTokenFilterPolicy /t REG_DWORD /d 1`. Learn more about access control. After failover, if you want connect to Windows virtual machines in Azure with Remote Desktop make sure that Remote Desktop is enabled for the on-premises machine. If you're not connecting over VPN, firewall rules should allow Remote Desktop connections over the internet.	
Linux machines	A supported 64 bit operating system: **Centos 6.4, 6.5, 6.6**; **Oracle Enterprise Linux 6.4, 6.5 running either the Red Hat compatible kernel or Unbreakable Enterprise Kernel Release 3 (UEK3)**, **SUSE Linux Enterprise Server 11 SP3**. Firewall rules on protected machines should allow them to reach the configuration and master target servers in Azure. /etc/hosts files on protected machines should contain entries that map the local host name to IP addresses associated with all NICs If you want to connect to an Azure virtual machine running Linux after failover using a Secure Shell client (ssh), ensure that the Secure Shell service on the protected machine is set to start automatically on system boot, and that firewall rules allow an ssh	

COMPONENT	REQUIREMENTS	DETAILS
	connection to it.	
	The host name, mount points, device names, and Linux system paths and file names (eg /etc/; /usr) should be in English only.	
	Protection can be enabled for on-premises machines with the following storage:- File system: EXT3, ETX4, ReiserFS, XFS Multipath software-Device Mapper (multipath) Volume manager: LVM2 Physical servers with HP CCISS controller storage are not supported.	
Third-party	Some deployment components in this scenario depend on third-party software to function properly. For a complete list see Third-party software notices and information	

Deployment

The graphic summarizes the deployment steps.

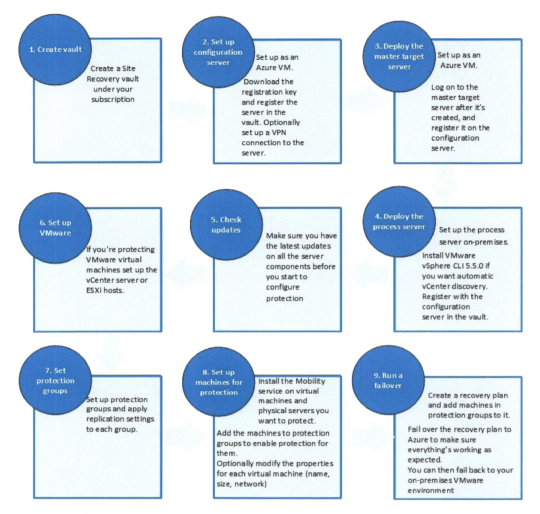

Network connectivity Type

You have two options to configure network connectivity between your on-premises site and the Azure virtual network on which your Infrastructure components (Configuration Server, Master target Servers) are deployed. You'll need to decide which network connectivity option to use before you can deploy your Configuration Server. This is a deployment time choice, and cannot be changed later.

Public Internet : Communication and replication of data between the on-premises servers (Process Server, Protected Servers) and the Azure Infrastructure component servers (Configuration Server, Master Target Server) happens over a secure SSL/TLS connection from on-premises to the Public endpoints on the Configuration Server and the Master Target server. (The only exception is the connection between the Process Server and the Master Target server on TCP port 9080 which is un-encrypted.

Only control information relatec to the replication protocol related used to setup the replication is exchanged on this connection.)

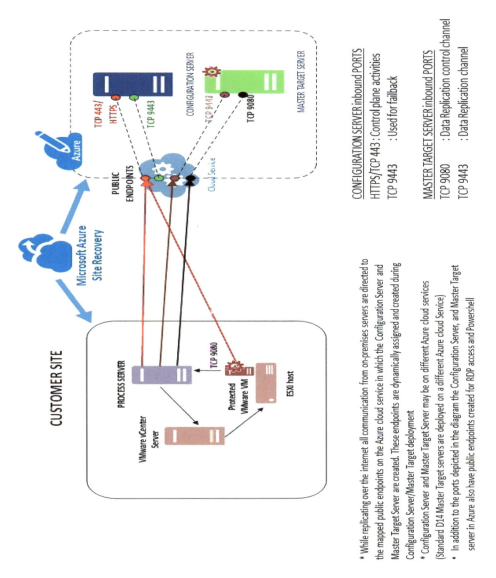

VPN : Communication and replication of data between the on-premises servers (Process Server, Protected Servers) and the Azure Infrastructure component servers (Configuration Server, Master Target Server) happens over a VPN connection between your on-premises network and the Azure virtual network on which the Configuration server and Master Target servers are deployed. Ensure that your on-premises network is connectec to the Azure virtual network by an ExpressRoute connection or a site-to-site VPN connection.

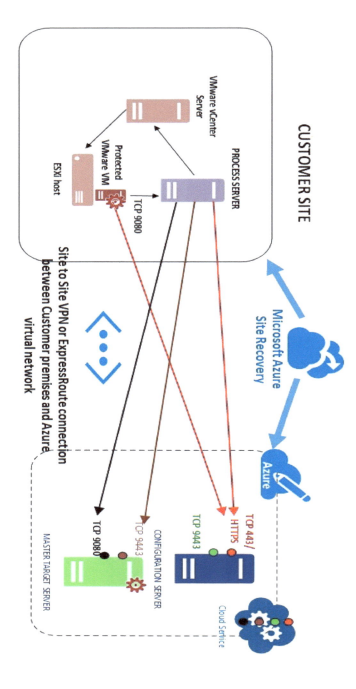

* While replicating over a VPN connection all communication from on-premises servers are directed to the internal ports on the Azure virtual network on which the Configuration Server and Master Target Server are connected.

* Configuration Server and Master Target Server may be on different Azure cloud services (Standard D14 Master Target servers are deployed on a different Azure cloud Service)

CONFIGURATION SERVER inbound PORTS
HTTPS/TCP 443 : Control plane activities
TCP 9443 : Used for failback

MASTER TARGET SERVER inbound PORTS
TCP 9080 : Data Replication control channel
TCP 9443 : Data Replication channel

Step 1: Create a vault

1.   Sign in to the Management Portal.

2.   Expand **Data Services** > **Recovery Services** and click **Site Recovery Vault**.

3.   Click **Create New** > **Quick Create**.

4.   In **Name**, enter a friend y name to identify the vault.

5.   In **Region**, select the geographic region for the vault. To check supported regions see Geographic Availability in Azure Site Recovery Pricing Details

6.   Click **Create vault**.

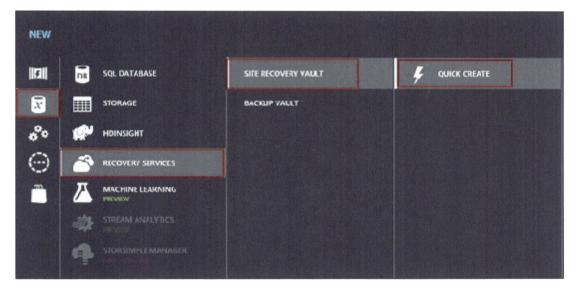

Check the status bar to confirm that the vault was successfully created. The vault will be listed as **Active** on the main **Recovery Services** page.

Step 2: Deploy a configuration server Configure server settings

1.   In the **Recovery Services** page, click the vault to ope the Quick Start page. Quick Start can also be opened at any time using the icon.

2.   In the dropdown list, select **Between an on-premises site with VMware/physical servers and Azure**.

3.   In **Prepare Target (Azure) Resources** click **Deploy Configuration Server**.

Prepare Target(Azure) Resources ⊘

After you deploy the Configuration Server, download and copy the registration key file to the Configuration Server. Launch the installer on the Configuration Server and use the key file to register the server to the vault. Generate registration key file creates a new key every time you click on it and only the latest key is valid at any given time. After the Configuration Server has been registered, deploy the Master Target Server. Once deployed, log in into the server and register it to the Configuration Server.

Deploy Configuration Server   Download a registration key

4.   In **New Configuration Server Details** specify:

- A name for the configuration server and credentials to connect to it.

- In the network connectivity type drop down select Public Internet or VPN. [AZURE.NOTE] This setting is a deployment time choice you make and cannot be changed later.

- Select the Azure network on which the server should be located. If you specified VPN as the network connectivity type ensure that this Azure vnet is connected to your on-premises site over an ExpressRoute connection or a site-to-site VPN.

- Specify the internal IP address and subnet to assign to the server. Note that the first four IP addresses in any subnet are reserved for internal Azure usage. Use any other available IP address.

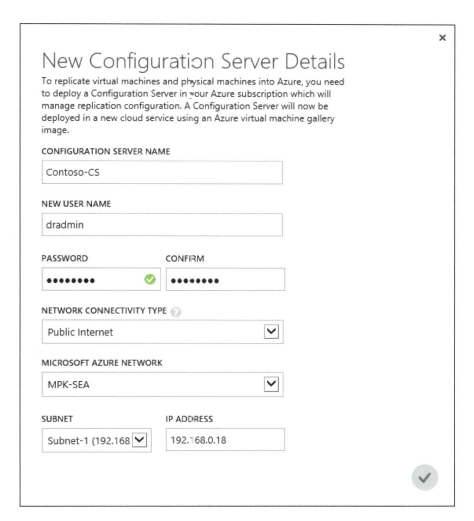

5.   When you click **OK** a standard A3 virtual machine based on an Azure Site Recovery Windows Server 2012 R2 gallery image will be created in your subscription for the configuration server. It's created as the first instance in a new cloud service. If you specified the network connectivity type to be Public Internet the cloud service is created with a reserved public IP address. You can monitor progress in the **Jobs** tab.

6. **This step is applicable only if your connectivity type is Public Internet.** After the configuration server is deployed note the public IP address assigned to it on the **Virtual Machines** page in the Azure portal. Then on the **Endpoints** tab note the public HTTPS port mapped to private port 443. You'll need this information later when you register the master target and process servers with the configuration server. The configuration server is deployed with these endpoints:

- HTTPS: Public port is used to coordinate communication between component servers and Azure over the internet. Private port 443 is used to coordinate communication between component servers and Azure over VPN.

- Custom: Public port is used for failback tool communication over the inter

- net. Private port 9443 is used for failback tool communication over VPN.

- PowerShell: Private port 5986

- Remote desktop: Private port 3389

WARNING:

Don't delete or change the public or private port number of any of the endpoints created during configuration server deployment.

The configuration server is deployed in an automatically created Azure cloud service with a reserved IP address. The reserved address is needed to ensure that the Configuration Server cloud service IP address remains the same across reboots of the virtual machines (including the configuration server) on the cloud service. The reserved public IP address will need to be manually unreserved when the configuration server is decommissioned or it'll remain reserved. There's a default limit of 20 reserved public IP addresses per subscription. Find out more about reserved IP addresses.

Register the configuration server in the vault

1. In the **Quick Start** page click **Prepare Target Resources** > **Download a registration key**. The key file is generated automatically. It's valid for 5 days after its generated. Copy it to the configuration server.

2. In **Virtual Machines** select the configuration server from the virtual machines list. Open the **Dashboard** tab and click **Connect**. **Open** the downloaded RDP file to log onto the configuration server using Remote Desktop. If your Configuration server is deployed on a VPN network, use the internal IP address (this is the IP address you specified when you deployed the configuration server and can also be seen on the virtual machines dashboard page for the configuration server virtual machine) of the configuration server to Remote desktop to it from your on-premises network. The Azure Site Recovery Configuration Server Setup Wizard runs automatically when you log on for the first time.

3. In **Third-Party Software Installation** click **I Accept** to download and install MySQL.

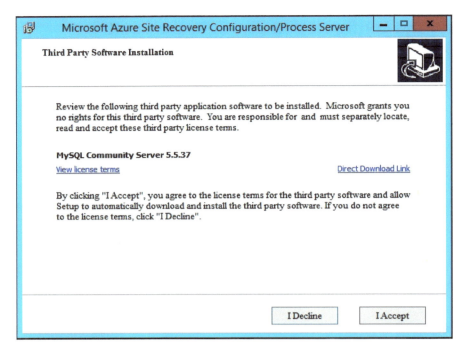

4. In **MySQL Server Details** create credentials to log onto the MySQL server instance.

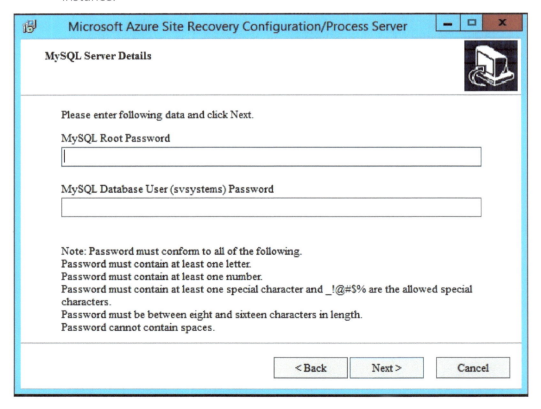

5. In **Internet Settings** specify how the configuration server will connect to the internet. Note that:

    - If you want to use a custom proxy you should set it up before you install the Provider.

    - When you click **Next** a test will run to check the proxy connection.

    - If you do use a custom proxy, or your default proxy requires authentication you ll need to enter the proxy details, including the address, port, and credentials.

    - The following URLs should be accessible via the proxy:

    *.hypervrecoverymanager.windowsazure.com
    *.accesscontrol.windows.net
    *.backup.windowsazure.com
    *.blob.core.windows.net
    *.store.core.windows.net

If you have IP address-based firewall rules ensure that the rules are set to allow communication from the configuration server to the IP addresses described in Azure Datacenter IP Ranges and HTTPS (443) protocol. You would have to white-list IP ranges of the Azure region that you plan to use, and that of West US.

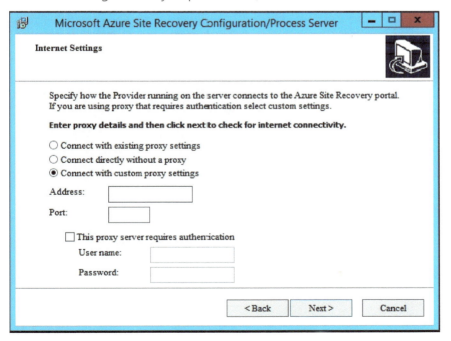

6. In **Provider Error Message Localization Settings** specify in which language you want error messages to appear.

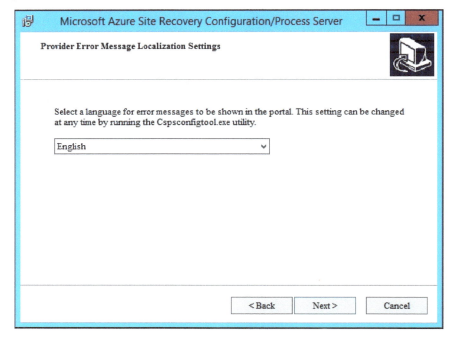

7. In **Azure Site Recovery Registration** browse and select the key file you copied to the server.

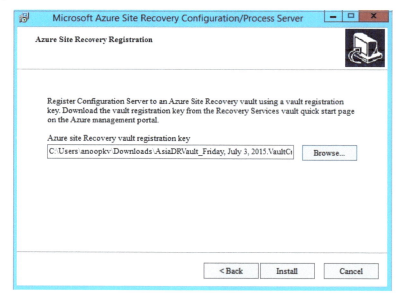

8. On the completion page of the wizard select these options:

- Select **Launch Account Management Dialog** to specify that the Manage Accounts dialog should open after you finish the wizard.

- Select **Create a desktop icon for Cspsconfigtool** to add a desktop shortcut on the configuration server so that you can open the **Manage Accounts**dialog at any time without needing to rerun the wizard.

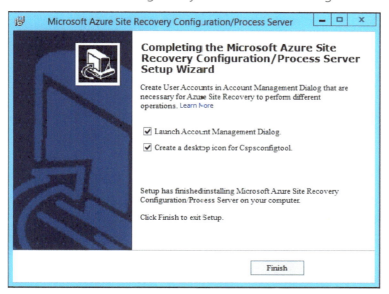

9. Click **Finish** to complete the wizard. A passphrase is generated. Copy it to a secure location. You'll need it to authenticate and register the process and master target servers with the configuration server. It's also used to ensure channel integrity in configuration server communications. You can regenerate the passphrase but then you'll need to re-register the master target and process servers using the new passphrase.

After registration the configuration server will be listed on the **Configuration Servers** page in the vault.

Set up and manage accounts

During deployment Site Recovery requests credentials for the following actions:

- When you add a vCenter server for automated discovery of virtual machines managed by the vCenter server. A vCenter account is required for automated discovery of virtual machines.

- When you add machines for protection, so that Site Recovery can install the Mobility service on them.

- After you've registered the configuration server you can open the **Manage Accounts** dialog to add and manage accounts that should be used for these actions. There are a couple of ways to do this:

- Open the shortcut you opted to create for the dialog on the last page of setup for the configuration server (cspsconfigtool).

- Open the dialog on finish of configuration server setup.

- In **Manage Accounts** click **Add Account**. You can also modify and delete existing accounts.

- In **Account Details** specify an account name to use in Azure and credentials (Domain/user name).

Connect to the configuration server

There are two ways to connect to the configuration server:

- Over a VPN site-to-site or ExpressRoute connection

- Over the internet

Note that:

- An internet connection uses the endpoints of the virtual machine in conjunction with the public virtual IP address of the server.

- A VPN connection uses the internal IP address of the server together with the endpoint private ports.

- It's a one-time decision to decide whether to connect (control and replication data) from your on-premises servers to the various component servers (configuration server, master target server) running in Azure over a VPN connection or the internet. You can't change this setting afterwards. If you do you'll need to redeploy the scenario and reprotect your machines.

Step 3: Deploy the master target server

1. In **Prepare Target (Azure) Resources**, click **Deploy master target server**.

2. Specify the master target server details and credentials. The server will be deployed in the same Azure network as the configuration server you register it to. When you click to complete an Azure virtual machine will be created with a Windows or Linux gallery image.

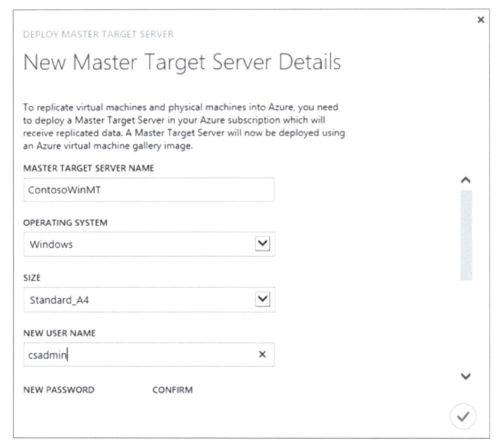

Note that the first four IP addresses in any subnet are reserved for internal Azure usage. Specify any other available IP address.

NOTE:

Select Standard DS4 when configuring protection for workloads which require consistent high IO performance and low latency in order to host IO intensive workloads using Premium Storage Account.

1. A Windows master target server virtual machine is created with these endpoints (Public endpoints are created only if your deployment type is Public Internet):

   * Custom: Public port is used by the process server to send replication data over the internet. Private port 9443 is used by the process server to send replication data to the master target server over VPN.

   * Custom1: Public port is used by the process server to send control meta-data over the internet. Private port 9080 is used by process server to send control meta-data to the master target server over VPN.

   * PowerShell: Private port 5986

   * Remote desktop: Private port 3389

2. A Linux master target server virtual machine is created with these endpoints (Public endpoints are created only if your deployment type is Public Internet):

   * Custom: Public port is used by the process server to send replication data over the internet. Private port 9443 is used by the process server to send replication data to the master target server over VPN.

   * Custom1: Public port is used by the process server to send control meta-data over the internet. Private port 9080 is used by the process server to send control data to the master target server over VPN

   * SSH: Private port 22

WARNING:

Don't delete or change the public or private port number of any of the endpoints created during the master target server deployment.

3. In **Virtual Machines** wait for the virtual machine to start.

   * If you've configured the server with Windows note down the remote desktop details.

   * If you configured with Linux and you're connecting over VPN note the internal IP address of the virtual machine. If you're connecting over the internet note the public IP address.

4. Log onto the server to complete installation and register it with the configuration server.

5. If you're running Windows:

- Initiate a remote desktop connection to the virtual machine. The first time you log on a script will run in a PowerShell window. Don't close it. When it finishes the Host Agent Config tool opens automatically to register the server.

- In **Host Agent Config** specify the internal IP address of the configuration server and port 443. You can use the internal address and private port 443 even if you're not connecting over VPN because the virtual machine is attached to the same Azure network as the configuration server. Leave **Use HTTPS** enabled. Enter the passphrase for the configuration server that you noted earlier. Click **OK** to register server. Note that you can ignore the NAT options on the page. They're not used.

- If your estimated retention drive requirement is more than 1 TB you can configure the retention volume (R:) using a virtual disk and **storage spaces**

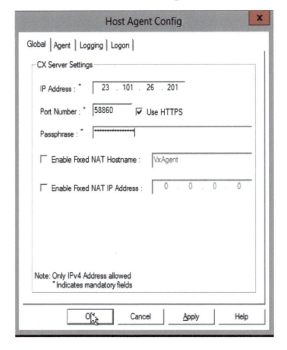

6. If you're running Linux:

   a. Ensure that you have installed the latest Linux Integration Services (LIS) installed before you install the Master target server software. You can find the latest version of LIS along with instructions on how to install here. Restart the machine after the LIS install.

b. In **Prepare Target(Azure) Resources** click **Download and Install additional software (only for Linux Master Target Server)** to download the Linux master target server package. Copy the downloaded tar file to the virtual machine using an sftp client. Alternatively you can log in to the deployed linux master target server and use *wget http://go.microsoft.com/fwlink/?LinkID=529757&clcid=0x409* to download the the file.

c. Log into the server using a Secure Shell client. Note that if you're connected to the Azure network over VPN use the internal IP address. Otherwise use the external IP address and the SSH public endpoint.

d. Extract the files from the gzipped installer by running: **tar –xvzf Microsoft-ASR_UA_8.4.0.0_RHEL6-64**

```
csadmin@ContosoLinMT1 ~]$
csadmin@ContosoLinMT1 ~]$ tar -xvzf Microsoft-ASR_UA_8.2.0.0_RHEL6-64_                    .tar.gz
```

e. Make sure you're in the directory to which you extracted the contents of the tar file.

f. Copy the configuration server passphrase to a local file using the command **echo** *<passphrase>* **>passphrase.txt**

g. Run the command "**sudo ./install -t both -a host -R MasterTarget -d /usr/local/ASR -i** *<Configuration server internal IP address>* **-p 443 -s y -c https -P passphrase.txt**".

```
dradmin@Fabrikam-LInMT:~                                              _  □  ×

[dradmin@Fabrikam-LInMT ~]$ echo "            " >passphrase.txt
[dradmin@Fabrikam-LInMT ~]$ sudo ./install -t both -a host -R MasterTarget -d /usr/l
ocal/ASR -i 10.0.0.10 -p 443 -s y -c https -P passphrase.txt
[sudo] password for dradmin:

Agent type of Installation is both
Agent Mode of Installation is host
Installation Directory is /usr/local/ASR
CX server IP address is 10.0.0.10
Communication mode is https
CX server Port number is 443
AGENT_ROLE is MasterTarget
To start the agent after installation is choosen as y
Passphrase file is passphrase.txt


Generating the certificate.

Validating the passphrase.

Passphrase validation is successful.
The chosen configuration for this VX is host based configuration...
Checking OS compatibility before installation...
```

h. Wait for a few minutes (10-15) and on the **Servers** > **Configuration Servers** page check that the master target server is listed as registered on the**Server Details** tab. If you're running Linux and it didn't register run the host config tool again from /usr/local/ASR/Vx/bin/hostconfigcli. You'll need to set access permissions by running chmod as root.

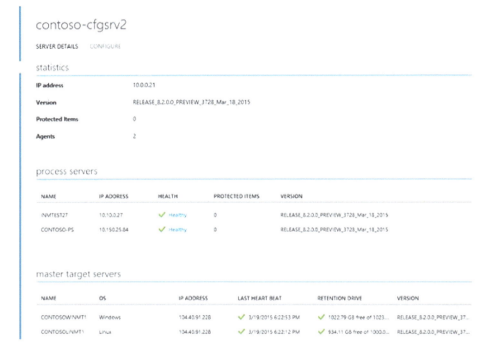

NOTE:

Please note that it can take up to 15 minutes after registration is complete for the master target server to be listed under the configuration server. To update immediately, refresh the configuration server by clicking on the refresh button at the bottom of the configuration servers page.

Step 4: Deploy the on-premises process server
NOTE:

We recommend that you configure a static IP address on the process server so that it's guaranteed to be persistent across reboots.

1. Click Quick Start > **Install Process Server on-premises** > **Download and install the process server**.

2 Prepare Process Servers ⊘

After deploying Process Server, register them with the Configuration Server.

Download and install Process Server   Learn how to deploy Process Server

2. Copy the downloaded zip file to the server on which you're going to install the process server. The zip file contains two installation files:

- Microsoft-ASR_CX_TP_8.4.0.0_Windows*

- Microsoft-ASR_CX_8.4.0.0_Windows*

3. Unzip the archive and copy the installation files to a location on the server.

4. Run the **Microsoft-ASR_CX_TP_8.4.0.0_Windows*** installation file and follow the instructions. This installs third-party components needed for the deployment.

5. Then run **Microsoft-ASR_CX_8.4.0.0_Windows***.

6. On the **Server Mode** page select **Process Server**.

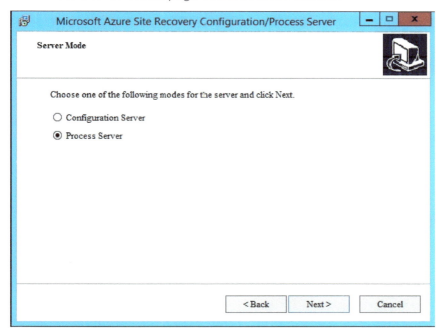

7. On the **Environment Detai s** page do the following:

- If you want to protect VMware virtual machines click **Yes**

- If you only want to protect physical servers and thus don't need VMware vCLI installed on the process server. Click **No** and continue.

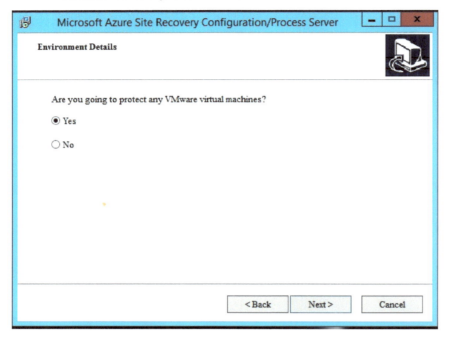

8. Note the following when installing VMware vCLI:

- **Only VMware vSphere CLI 5.5.0 is supported**. The process server doesn't work with other versions or updates of vSphere CLI.

- Download vSphere CLI 5.5.0 from here.

- If you installed vSphere CLI just before you started installing the process server, and setup doesn't detect it, wait up to five minutes before you try setup again. This ensures that all the environment variables needed for vSphere CLI detection have been initialized correctly.

9. In **NIC Selection for Process Server** select the network adapter that the process server should use.

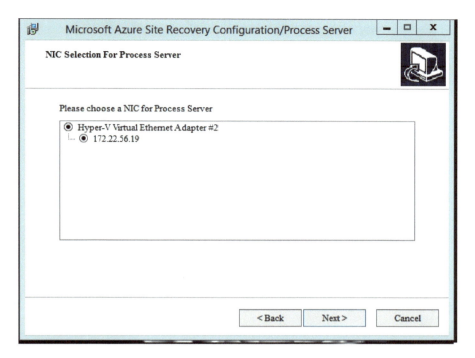

10. In **Configuration Server Details**:

- For the IP address and port, if you're connecting over VPN specify the internal IP address of the configuration server and 443 for the port. Otherwise specify the public virtual IP address and mapped public HTTP endpoint.

- Type in the passphrase of the configuration server.

- Clear **Verify Mobility service software signature** if you want to disable verification when you use automatic push to install the service. Signature verification needs internet connectivity from the process server.

- Click **Next**.

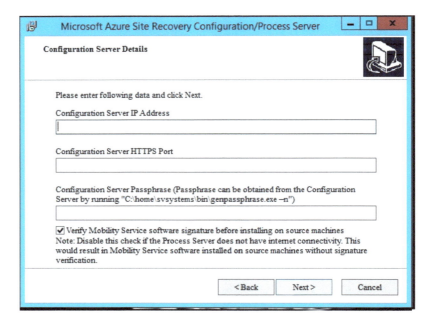

11. In **Select Installation Drive** select a cache drive. The process server needs a cache drive with at least 600 GB of free space. Then click **Install**.

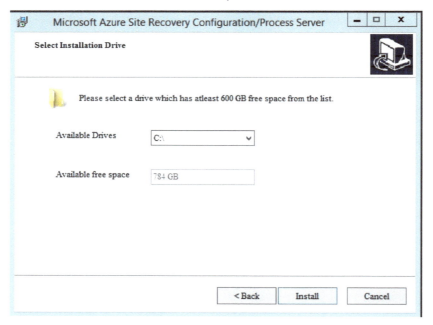

12. Note that you might need to restart the server to complete the installation. In **Configuration Server** > **Server Details** check that the process server appears and is registered successfully in the vault.

NOTE:

It can take up to 15 minutes after registration is complete for the process server to appear as listed under the configuration server. To update immediately, refresh the configuration server by clicking on the refresh button at the bottom of the configuration server page

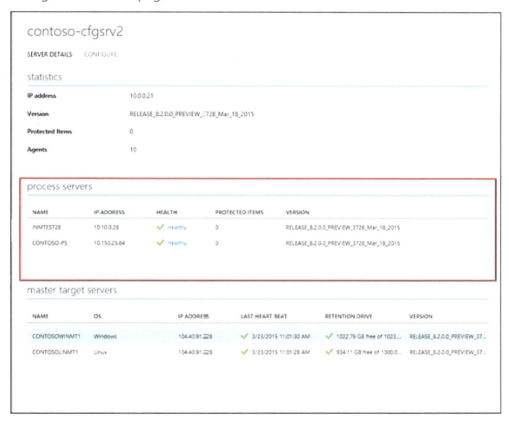

If you didn't disable signature verification for the Mobility service when you registered the process server you can do it later as follows:

13. Log onto the process server as an administrator and open the file C:\pushinstallsvc\pushinstaller.conf for editing. Under the section**[PushInstaller.transport]** add this line: **SignatureVerificationChecks="0"**. Save and close the file.

14. Restart the InMage PushInstall service.

Step 5: Install latest updates

Before proceeding, ensure that you have the latest updates installed. **Remember to install the updates in the Following order ONLY:**

1. Configuration server

2. Process server

3. Master target server

You can get the updates on the Site Recovery **Dashboard **. For Linux installation extract the files from the gzipped installer and run the command "sudo ./install" to install the update

If you are running virtual machines or physical servers that already have the Mobility service installed, you can get updates for the service as follows:

Either download updates for the service as follows: (*For those using hard copy of the book, please search in Google for the last part (file name) in the link*).

*   Windows Server (64 bit only)

    http://download.microsoft.com/download/8/4/8/8487F25A-E7D9-4810-99E4-6C18DF13A6D3/Microsoft-ASR_UA_8.4.0.0_Windows_GA_28Jul2015_release.exe

*   CentOS 6.4,6.5,6.6 (64 bit only)

    http://download.microsoft.com/download/7/E/D/7ED50614-1FE1-41F8-B4D2-25D73F623E9B/Microsoft-ASR_UA_8.4.0.0_RHEL6-64_GA_28Jul2015_release.tar.gz

*   Oracle Enterprise Linux 6.4,6.5 (64 bit only)

    http://download.microsoft.com/download/5/2/6/526AFE4B-7280-4DC6-B10B-BA3FD18B8091/Microsoft-ASR_UA_8.4.0.0_OL6-64_GA_28Jul2015_release.tar.gz

*   SUSE Linux Enterprise Server SP3 (64 bit only)

    http://download.microsoft.com/download/B/4/2/B4229162-C25C-4DB2-AD40-D0AE90F92305/Microsoft-ASR_UA_8.4.0.0_SLES11-SP3-64_GA_28Jul2015_release.tar.gz

*   Alternatively after updating the process server you can get the updated version of the Mobility service from the C:\pushinstallsvc\repository folder on the process server.

- If you have an already protected machine with an older version of the Mobility service installed, you could also automatically upgrade the Mobility service on the protected machines from the management portal. To do this, select the protection group to which the machine belongs, highlight the protected machine and click on the Update Mobility service button at the bottom. The Update Mobility Service button will be activated only if a newer version of the Mobility Service is available. Please ensure that the Process server is running the latest version of the Process server software before updating the mobility service. The protected server needs to meet all the automatic push-installation prerequisites in order for update mobility service to work.

- In Select accounts specify the administrator account to be used to update the mobility service on the protected server. Click OK and wait for the triggered job to complete.

Step 6: Add vCenter servers or ESXi hosts

1. On the **Servers** > **Configuration Servers** tab select the configuration server and click **ADD VCENTER SERVER** to add a vCenter server or ESXi host.

2. Specify details for the vCenter server or ESXi host and select the process server that will be used to discover it.

• If the vCenter server isn't running on the default 443 port specify the port number on which the vCenter server is running.

• The process server must be on the same network as the vCenter server/ESXi host and should have VMware vSphere CLI 5.5.0 installed.

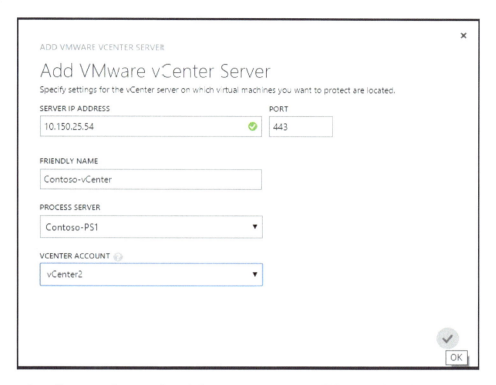

3. After discovery is completed the vCenter server will be listed under the configuration server details.

4. If you're using a non-administrator account to add the vCenter server or ESXi host, make sure the account has the following privileges:

- vCenter accounts should have Datacenter, Datastore, Folder, Host, Network, Resource, Storage views, Virtual machine and vSphere Distributed Switch privileges enabled.

- ESXi host accounts should have the Datacenter, Datastore, Folder, Host, Network, Resource, Virtual machine and vSphere Distributed Switch privileges enabled

Step 7: Create a protection group

1. Open **Protected Items** > **Protection Group** and click to add a protection group.

2. On the **Specify Protection Group Settings** page specify a name for the group and select the configuration server on which you want to create the group.

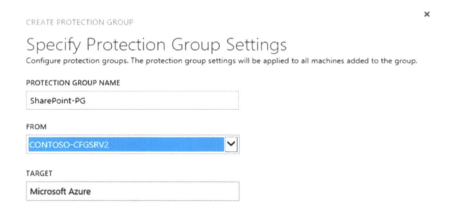

3. On the **Specify Replication Settings** page configure the replication settings that will be used for all the machines in the group.

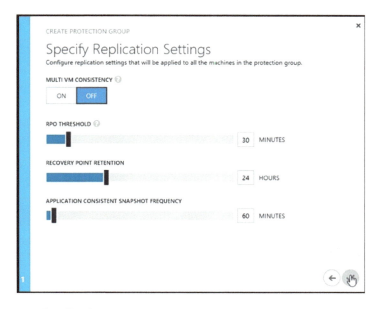

4. Settings:

*   **Multi VM consistency**: If you turn this on it creates shared application-consistent recovery points across the machines in the protection group. This setting is most relevant when all of the machines in the protection group are running the same workload. All machines will be recovered to the same data point. Only available for Windows servers.

*   **RPO threshold**: Alerts will be generated when the continuous data protection replication RPO exceeds the configured RPO threshold value.

*   **Recovery point retention**: Specifies the retention window. Protected machines can be recovered to any point within this window.

*   **Application-consistent snapshot frequency**: Specifies how frequently recovery points containing application-consistent snapshots will be created.

*   You can monitor the protection group as they're created on the **Protected Items** page.

Step 8: Set up machines you want to protect

You'll need to install the Mobility service on virtual machines and physical servers you want to protect. You can do this in two ways:

*   Automatically push and install the service on each machine from the process server.

- Manually install the service.

Install the Mobility service automatically

When you add machines to a protection group the Mobility service is automatically pushed and installed on each machine by the process server.

Automatically push install the mobility service on Windows servers:

1. Install the latest updates for the process server as described in Step 5: Install latest updates, and make sure that the process server is available.

2. Ensure there's network connectivity between the source machine and the process server, and that the source machine is accessible from the process server.

3. Configure the Windows firewall to allow **File and Printer Sharing** and **Windows Management Instrumentation**. Under Windows Firewall settings, select the option "Allow an app or feature through Firewall" and select the applications as shown in the picture below. For machines that belong to a domain you can configure the firewall policy with a Group Policy Object.

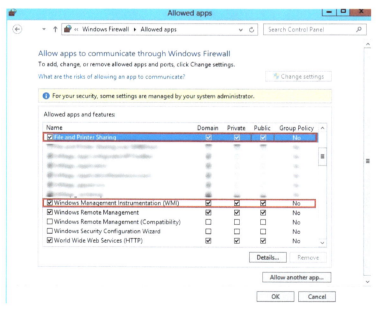

4. The account used to perform the push installation must be in the Administrators group on the machine you want to protect. These credentials are only used for push installation of the Mobility service and you'll provide them when you add a machine to a protection group.

5. If the provided account isn't a domain account you'll need to disable Remote User Access control on the local machine. To do this add the LocalAccountTokenFilterPolicy DWORD registry entry with a value of 1 under HKEY_LOCAL_MACHINE\SOFTWARE\Microsoft\Windows\CurrentVersion\Policies\System. To add the registry entry from a CLI open cmd or powershell and enter `REG ADD HKEY_LOCAL_MACHINE\SOFTWARE\Microsoft\Windows\CurrentVersion\Policies\System /v LocalAccountTokenFilterPolicy /t REG_DWORD /d 1`.

Automatically push install the mobility service on Linux servers:

1. Install the latest updates for the process server as described in Step 5: Install latest updates, and make sure that the process server is available.

2. Ensure there's network connectivity between the source machine and the process server, and that the source machine is accessible from the process server.

3. Make sure the account s a root user on the source Linux server.

4. Ensure that the /etc/hosts file on the source Linux server contains entries that map the local host name to IP addresses associated with all NICs.

5. Install the latest openssh, openssh-server, openssl packages on the machine you want to protect.

6. Ensure SSH is enabled and running on port 22.

7. Enable SFTP subsystem and password authentication in the sshd_config file as follows:

   a. Log in as root.

   b. In the file /etc/ssh/sshd_config file, find the line that begins with **PasswordAuthentication**.

   c. Uncomment the line and change the value from "no" to "yes".

   d.
   ```
   # To disable tunneled clear text passwords, change to no here!
   PasswordAuthentication yes
   ```

   e. Find the line that begins with Subsystem and uncomment the line.

```
# override default of no subsystems
Subsystem        sftp    /usr/libexec/openssh/sftp-server
```

8. Ensure the source machine Linux variant is supported.

Install the Mobility service manually

The software packages used to install the Mobility service are on the process server in C:\pushinstallsvc\repository. Log onto the process server and copy the appropriate installation package to the source machine based on the table below:-

SOURCE OPERATING SYSTEM	MOBILITY SERVICE PACKAGE ON PROCESS SERVER
Windows Server (64 bit only)	C:\pushinstallsvc\repository\Microsoft-ASR_UA_8.4.0.0_Windows_GA_28Jul2015_release.exe
CentOS 6.4, 6.5, 6.6 (64 bit only)	C:\pushinstallsvc\repository\Microsoft-ASR_UA_8.4.0.0_RHEL6-64_GA_28Jul2015_release.tar.gz
SUSE Linux Enterprise Server 11 SP3 (64 bit only)	C:\pushinstallsvc\repository\Microsoft-ASR_UA_8.4.0.0_SLES11-SP3-64_GA_28Jul2015_release.tar.gz
Oracle Enterprise Linux 6.4, 6.5 (64 bit only)	C:\pushinstallsvc\repository\Microsoft-ASR_UA_8.4.0.0_OL6-64_GA_28Jul2015_release.tar.gz

To install the Mobility service manually on a Windows server, do the following:

1. Copy the :

    Microsoft-ASR_UA_8.4.0.0_Windows_GA_28Jul2015_release.exe package from the process server directory path listed in the table above to the source machine.

2. Install the Mobility service by running the executable on the source machine.

3. Follow the installer instructions.

4. Select **Mobility service** as the role and click **Next**.

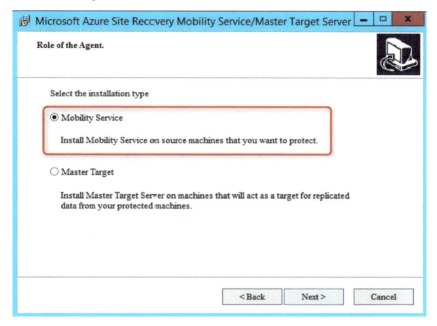

5. Leave the installation directory as the default installation path and click **Install**.

6. In **Host Agent Config** specify the IP address and HTTPS port of the configuration server.

- If you're connecting over the internet specify the public virtual IP address and public HTTPS endpoint as the port.

- If you're connecting over VPN specify the internal IP address and 443 for the port. Leave **Use HTTPS** checked.

7. Specify the configuration server passphrase and click **OK** to register the Mobility service with the configuration server.

To run from the command line:

8. Copy the passphrase from the CX to the file "C:\connection.passphrase" on the server and run this command. In our example CX i 104.40.75.37 and the HTTPS port is 62519:

```
C:\Microsoft-ASR_UA_8.2.0.0_Windows_PREVIEW_20Mar2015_Release.exe" -ip
104.40.75.37 -port 62519 -mode UA /LOG="C:\stdout.txt" /DIR="C:\Program Files
(x86)\Microsoft Azure Site Recovery" /VERYSILENT /SUPPRESSMSGBOXES /norestart -
usesysvolumes /CommunicationMode https /PassphrasePath
"C:\connection.passphrase"
```

Install the Mobility service manually on a Linux server:

1. Copy the appropriate tar archive based on the table above, from the process server to the source machine.

2. Open a shell program and extract the zipped tar archive to a local path by executing tar -xvzf Microsoft-ASR_UA_8.2.0.0*

3. Create a passphrase.txt file in the local directory to which you extracted the contents of the tar archive by entering *echo <passphrase> >passphrase.txt*from shell.

4. Install the Mobility service by entering *sudo ./install -t both -a host -R Agent -d /usr/local/ASR -i <IP address> -p <port> -s y -c https -P passphrase.txt.*

5. Specify the IP address and port:

   - If you are connecting to the configuration server over the internet specify the configuration server virtual public IP address and public HTTPS endpoint in <IP address> and <port>.

   - If you're connecting over a VPN connection specify the internal IP address and 443.

To run from the command line:

1. Copy the passphrase from the CX to the file "passphrase.txt" on the server and run this commands In our example CX i 104.40.75.37 and the HTTPS port is 62519:

To install on a production server:

Copy

```
./install -t both -a host -R Agent -d /usr/local/ASR -i 104.40.75.37 -p 62519 -s
y -c https -P passphrase.txt
```

To install on the target server:

Copy

```
./install -t both -a host -R MasterTarget -d /usr/local/ASR -i 104.40.75.37 -p
62519 -s y -c https -P passphrase.txt
```

NOTE:

When you add machines to a protection group that are already running an appropriate version of the Mobility service then the push installation is skipped.

Step 9: Enable Protection

- To enable protection you add virtual machines and physical servers to a protection group. Before you start, note that:

- Virtual machines are discovered every 15 minutes and it can take up to 15 minutes for them to appear in Azure Site Recovery after discovery.

- Environment changes on the virtual machine (such as VMware tools installation) can also take up to 15 minutes to be updated in Site Recovery.

- You can check the last discovered time in the **LAST CONTACT AT** field for the vCenter server/ESXi host on the **Configuration Servers** page.

- If you have a protection group already created and add a vCenter Server or ESXi host after that, it takes fifteen minutes for the Azure Site Recovery portal to refresh and for virtual machines to be listed in the **Add machines to a protection group** dialog.

- If you would like to proceed immediately with adding machines to protection group without waiting for the scheduled discovery, highlight the configuration server (don't click it) and click the **Refresh** button.

- When you add virtual machines or physical machines to a protection group, the process server automatically pushes and installs the Mobility service on the source server if the it isn't already installed.

For the automatic push mechanism to work make sure you've set up your protected machines as described in the previous step.

<u>Add machines as follows:</u>

1. **Protected Items** > **Protection Group** > **Machines** tab. Click **ADD MACHINES**. As a best practice we recommend that protection groups should mirror your workloads so that you add machines running a specific application to the same group.

2. In **Select Virtual Machines** if you're protecting physical servers, in the **Add Physical Machines** wizard provide the IP address and friendly name. Then select the operating system family.

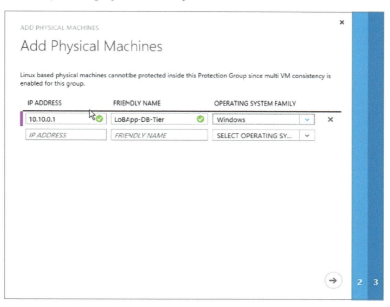

3. In **Select Virtual Machines** if you're protecting VMware virtual machines, select a vCenter server that's managing your virtual machines (or the EXSi host on which they're running), and then select the machines.

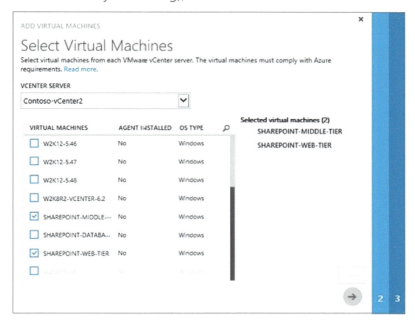

4. In **Specify Target Resources** select the master target servers and storage to use for replication and select whether the settings should be used for all workloads. Select Premium Storage Account while configuring protection for workloads which require consistent high IO performance and low latency in order to host IO intensive workloads. If you want to use a Premium Storage account for your workload disks, you need to use the Master Target of DS-series. You cannot use Premium Storage disks with Master Target of non-DS-series.

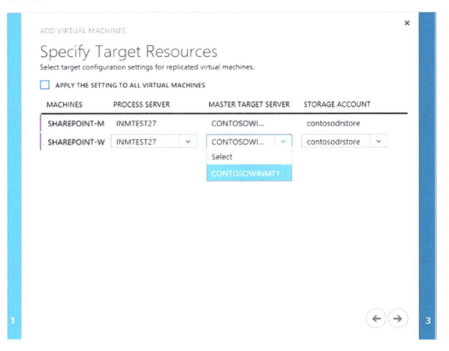

5. In **Specify Accounts** select the account you want to use for installing the Mobility service on protected machines. The account credentials are needed for automatic installation of the Mobility service. If you can't select an account make sure you set one up as described in Step 2. Note that this account can't be accessed by Azure. For Windows server the account should have administrator privileges on the source server. For Linux the account must be root.

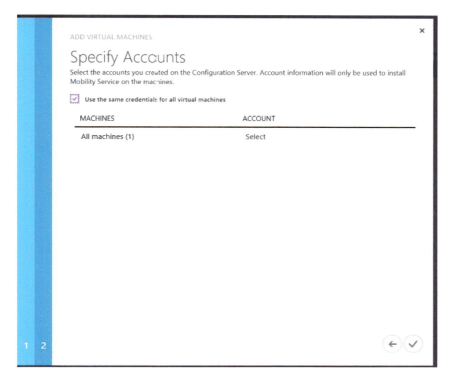

6. Click the check mark to finish adding machines to the protection group and to start initial replication for each machine. You can monitor status on the **Jobs** page.

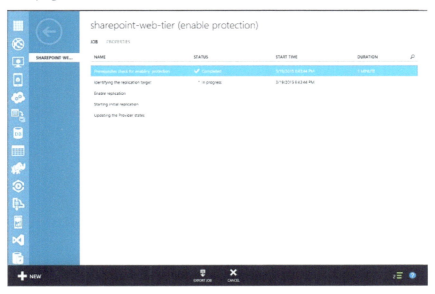

7. In addition you can monitor protection status by clicking **Protected Items** > protection group name > **Virtual Machines** . After initial replication

completes and the machines are synchronizing data they will show **Protected** status.

Set protected machine properties

1. After a machine has a **Protected** status you can configure its failover properties. In the protection group details select the machine and open the**Configure** tab.

2. You can modify the name that will be given to the machine in Azure after failover and the Azure virtual machine size. You can also select the Azure network to which the machine will be connected after failover.

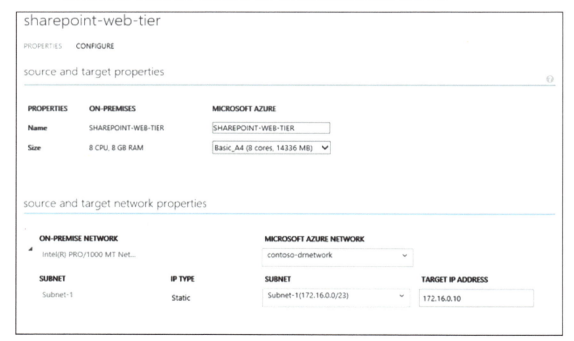

Note that:

The name of the Azure machine must comply with Azure requirements.

- By default replicated virtual machines in Azure aren't connected to an Azure network. If you want replicated virtual machines to communicate make sure to set the same Azure network for them.

- If you resize a volume on a VMware virtual machine or physical server it goes into a critical state. If you do need to modify the size, do the following:

- Change the size setting.

- In the **Virtual Machines** tab, select the virtual machine and click **Remove**.

- In **Remove Virtual Machine** select the option **Disable protection (use for recovery drill and volume resize)**. This option disables protection but retains the recovery points in Azure.

- Reenable protection for the virtual machine. When you reenable protection the data for the resized volume will be transferred to Azure.

Step 10: Run a failover

- Currently you can only run unplanned failovers for protected VMware virtual machines and physical servers. Note the following:

- Before you initiate a failover, ensure that the configuration and master target servers are running and healthy. Otherwise failover will fail.

- Source machines aren't shut down as part of an unplanned failover. Performing an unplanned failover stops data replication for the protected servers. You'll need to delete the machines from the protection group and add them again in order to start protecting machines again after the unplanned failover completes.

- If you want to fail over without losing any data, make sure that the primary site virtual machines are turned off before you initiate the failover.

- On the **Recovery Plans** page and add a recovery plan. Specify details for the plan and select **Azure** as the target.

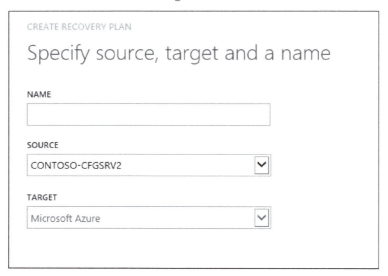

- In **Select Virtual Machine** select a protection group and then select machines in the group to add to the recovery plan. Read more about recovery plans.

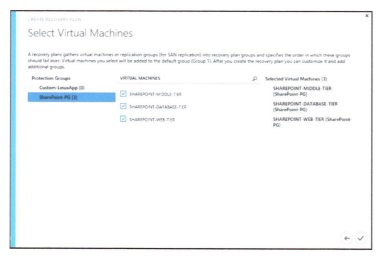

- If needed you can customize the plan to create groups and sequence the order in which machines in the recovery plan are failed over. You can also add prompts for manual actions and scripts. The scripts when recovering to Azure can be added by using Azure Automation Runbooks.

- In the **Recovery Plans** page select the plan and click **Unplanned Failover**.

- In **Confirm Failover** verify the failover direction (To Azure) and select the recovery point to fail over to.

- Wait for the failover job to complete and then verify that the failover worked as expected and that the replicated virtual machines start successfully in Azure.

Step 11: Fail back failed over machines from Azure

After a successful failover to Azure, the virtual machines will be available in the virtual machines tab. When you decide to failback – below are the steps you need to follow.

I am giving the steps for failback to VMware as its third party to Microsoft products and Hyper-V is more simple and straight forward especially if VMM is installed.

Note that when you failback from Azure back to your VMware site, the recovery can only be to a virtual machine. Even if your initial source on VMware was a physical machine, failover to Azure followed by a failback to VMware will convert it into a virtual machine.

Overview

1. Install vContinuum server on-premises
2. Configure it to point to the CS
3. Deploy a PS on Azure
4. Install a MT on-premises
5. Steps to protect the failed over VMs back to on-premises
6. Configuration considerations
7. Monitoring protection of VMs back to on-premises
8. Failover the VMs back to on-premises

Below is the setup overview that we will achieve with the below steps. Part of the setup has already been completed during failover.

- The blue lines are the connections used during failover.

- The red lines are the connections used during failback.

- The lines with arrows go over the internet.

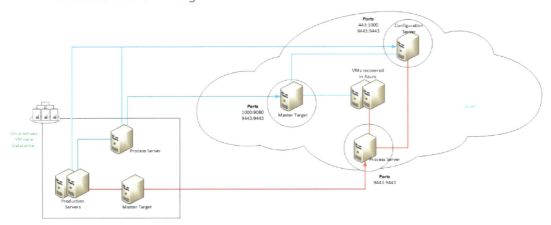

Install vContinuum on-premises

The vContinuum setup will be at available at Microsoft download location. In addition install the patch given here on the vContinuum - available at download location.

1. Launch the setup to begin installation of vContinuum. Click **Next**.

2. Specify the CX server IP address and the CX server port. Select HTTPS.

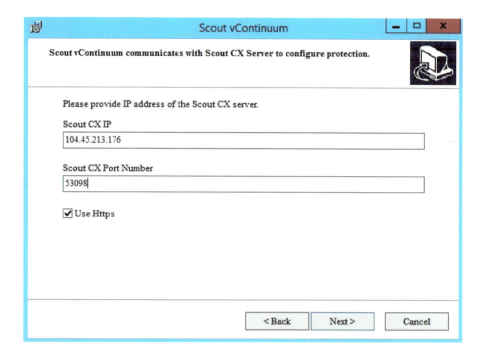

3. To discover the CX IP address go to the CS deployment on Azure and view its dashboard.

4. To discover the CX public port go to the endpoints tab in the VM page and identify the HTTPs endpoints public port.

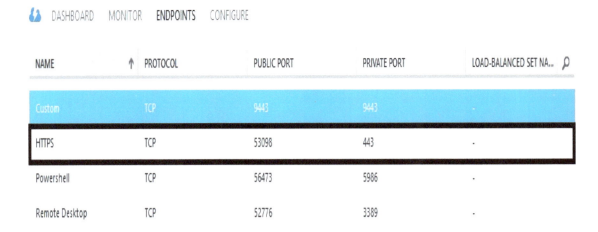

DASHBOARD   MONITOR   **ENDPOINTS**   CONFIGURE

NAME	↑	PROTOCOL	PUBLIC PORT	PRIVATE PORT	LOAD-BALANCED SET NA...
Custom		TCP	9443	9443	-
HTTPS		TCP	53098	443	-
Powershell		TCP	56473	5986	-
Remote Desktop		TCP	52776	3389	-

5. Specify the CS Passphrase. You need to have noted down the passphrase during the CS registration. You would have used the passphrase during MT and PS deployments also. In case you do not remember the passphrase you can go in to the CS server on Azure and find the passphrase stored under C:\Program Files (x86)\InMage Systems\private\connection.passphrase

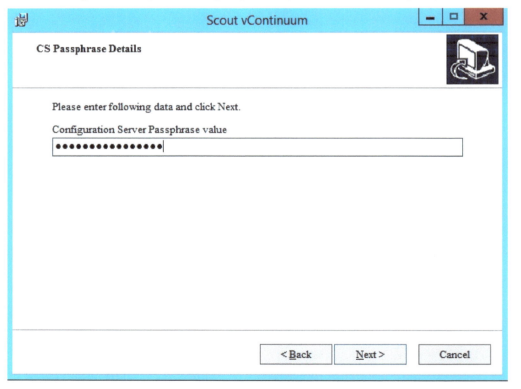

6. Specify the location to install the vContinuum server and begin installation.

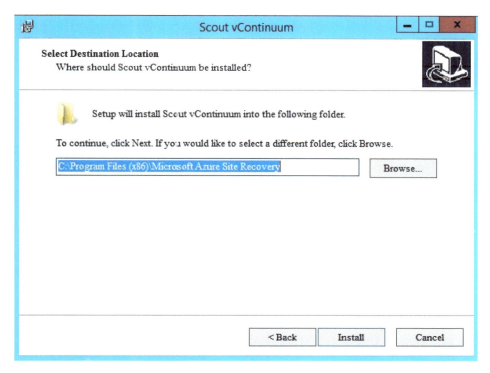

7. Once you see that installation completes, you can launch the vContinuum to see it working.

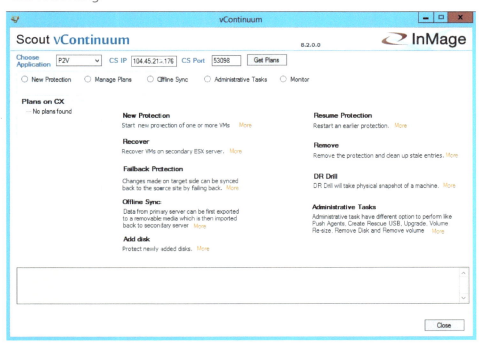

Install PS server on Azure

A Process Server needs to be installed on Azure so that the VMs in Azure can send the data back to on-premises MT. You need to deploy the PS on Azure in the same network as the Configuration Server.

8. On the **Configuration Servers** page in Azure, select to add a new process server.

9. Specify a process server name, and enter a name and password to connect to the virtual machine as an admin. Select the configuration server to which you're registering the process server. This should be the same server you're using to protect and fail over your virtual machines. Specify the Azure ntwork in which the process server should be deployment. It should be the same network as the configuration server. Specify a unique IP address from the select subnet and begin deployment.

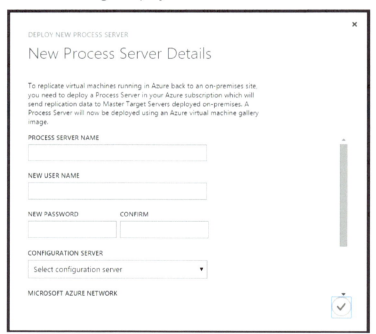

A job to deploy the process server will be triggered.

Once the process server is deplcyed on Azure you can log into the server using the credentials you specified. Use the same steps you used during forward direction of protection to register the PS.

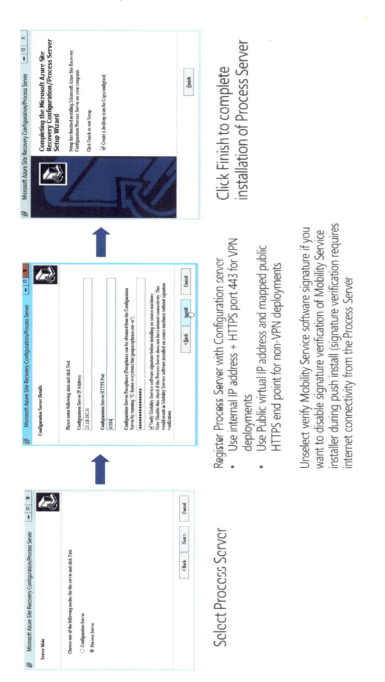

Select Process Server

Register Process Server with Configuration server
- Use internal IP address + HTTPS port 443 for VPN deployments
- Use Public virtual IP address and mapped public HTTPS end point for non-VPN deployments

Unselect verify Mobility Service software signature if you want to disable signature verification of Mobility Service installer during push install (signature verification requires internet connectivity from the Process Server

Click Finish to complete installation of Process Server

The servers registered during failback will not be visible under VM properties. They will be only visible under the Servers tab under the Configuration server to which they have been registered. It can take about 10-15 mins for the PS to be listed under the CS.

Install an MT server on-premises

Depending on the source side virtual machines you need to install Linux or a Windows Master Target server on-premises.

Deploy Windows MT

A windows MT is already bundled with vContinuum setup. When you install the vContinuum, an MT is also deployed on the same machine and registered to the Configuration server.

1. To begin deployment, create an empty machine on-premises on the ESX host onto which you want to recover the VMs from Auzre.

2. Ensure that there are at least two disks attached to the VM – one is used for the OS and the second one is used for Retention Drive.

3. Install the operating system.

4. Install the vContinuum on the server. This would also complete installation of the MT.

Deploy Linux MT

1. To begin deployment, create an empty machine on-premises on the ESX host onto which you want to recover the VMs from Auzre.

2. Ensure that there are at least two disks attached to the VM – one is used for the OS and the second one is used for Retention Drive.

3. Install the linux operating system. NLinux Master Target (MT) system should not use LVM for root or retention storage spaces. Linux MT configured to avoid LVM partitions/disks discovery by default.

4. Partitions that you can create are

Partition Name	Partition size allocation formula	FS Type
/	32GB	ext4
/var/crash	Total (RAM size + 20% of the RAM)	ext4
swap	Minimum (double of the RAM size or 32GB)	swap
/home	Entire remaining space	ext4

5. Carry out the below post installation steps before beginning MT installation.

Post OS Installation Steps

To get SCSI ID's for each of SCSI hard disk in a Linux virtual machine, you should enable the parameter "disk.EnableUUID = TRUE". To enable this parameter, follow the steps as given below:

1. Shut down your virtual machine.

2. Right-click the VM's entry in the left-hand panel > **Edit Settings**.

3. Click the **Options** tab. Select the **Advanced>General item** on the left and click the **Configuration Parameters** that you see on the right. "Configuration Parameters" option will be in de-active state when the machine is running". In order to make this tab active, shutdown machine.

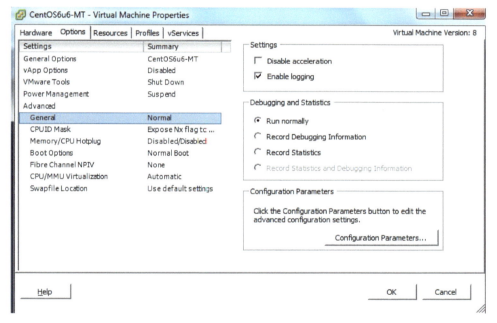

4. See whether already a row with **disk.EnableUUID** exists? If exists and if the value is set to False over write the value with True (True and False values are case in-sensitive). If exists and is set to true, click on cancel and test the SCSI command inside guest operating system after it is boot-up. If does not exist click **Add Row.**

5. Add disk.EnableUUID in the Name column. Set its value as TRUE. Do not add the above values along with double-quotes.

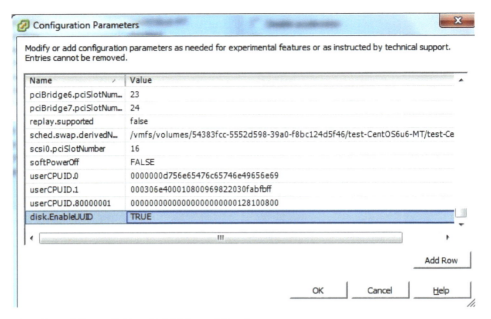

Download and Install the Additional Packages

NOTE: Make sure system has Internet connectivity before download and installing additional packages.

yum install -y xfsprogs perl lsscsi rsync wget kexec-tools

Above command will download below mentioned 15 packages from CentOS 6.6 repository and install.

bc-1.06.95-1.el6.x86_64.rpm

busybox-1.15.1-20.el6.x86_64.rpm

elfutils-libs-0.158-3.2.el6.x86_64.rpm

kexec-tools-2.0.0-280.el6.x86_64.rpm

lsscsi-0.23-2.el6.x86_64.rpm

lzo-2.03-3.1.el6_5.1.x86_64.rpm

perl-5.10.1-136.el6_6.1.x86_64.rpm

perl-Module-Pluggable-3.90-136.el6_6.1.x86_64.rpm

perl-Pod-Escapes-1.04-136.el6_6.1.x86_64.rpm

perl-Pod-Simple-3.13-136.el6_6.1.x86_64.rpm

perl-libs-5.10.1-136.el6_6.1.x86_64.rpm

perl-version-0.77-136.el6_6.1.x86_64.rpm

rsync-3.0.6-12.el6.x86_64.rpm

snappy-1.1.0-1.el6.x86_64.rpm

wget-1.12-5.el6_6.1.x86_64.rpm

NOTE: If source machine uses Reiser or XFS filesystem for root or boot device, then following packages should be download and installed on Linux Master Target prior to the protection.

cd /usr/local

wget http://elrepo.org/linux/e repo/el6/x86_64/RPMS/kmod-reiserfs-0.0-1.el6.elrepo.x86_64.rpm

wget http://elrepo.org/linux/e repo/el6/x86_64/RPMS/reiserfs-utils-3.6.21-1.el6.elrepo.x86_64.rpm

rpm -ivh kmod-reiserfs-0.0-1.el6.elrepo.x86_64.rpm reiserfs-utils-3.6.21-1.el6.elrepo.x86_64.rpm

wget http://mirror.centos.org/centos/6.6/os/x86_64/Packages/xfsprogs-3.1.1-16.el6.x86_64.rpm

rpm -ivh xfsprogs-3.1.1-16.el6.x86_64.rpm

Apply Custom Configuration Changes

Before applying custom configuration changes make sure you have completed Post Installation Steps

To apply custom configuration changes, follow the below mentioned steps:

1. Copy the RHEL 6-64 Unified Agent binary to the newly created OS.

2. Run the below command to un-tar the binary.

   tar -zxvf <File name>

3. Execute below command to give permission.

   # **chmod 755 ./ApplyCustomChanges.sh**

4. Execute the below command to run the script.

   # **./ApplyCustomChanges.sh**

   NOTE: Execute the script only once on the server. **REBOOT** the server after successful execution of the above script.

5. Begin MT Installation

Download the Linux Master Target Server installation file from the below link.

http://go.microsoft.com/fwlink/?LinkID=529757

1. Copy the downloaded Linux Master Target Server installer to the Linux Master Target virtual machine using an sftp client utility of your choice. Alternately you can log into the Linux Master Target virtual machine and use wget to download the installation package from the provided link.

2. Log in to the Linux Master Target server virtual machine using an ssh client of your choice.

3. If you are connected to the Azure network on which you deployed your Linux Master Target server through a VPN connection then use the internal IP address for the Linux Master Target Server obtained from the virtual machine dashboard and port 22 to connect to the Linux Master Target Server using Secure Shell.

4. If you are connecting to the Linux Master Target Server over a public internet connection use the Linux Master Target Server's public virtual IP address (from the virtual machines dashboard page) and the public endpoint created for ssh to login to the Linux Master Target Server.

5. Extract the files from the gzipped Linux Master Target Server installer tar archive by executing

"tar –xvzf Microsoft-ASR_UA_8.2.0.0_RHEL6-64"* from the directory where you had copied the Linux Master Target Server installer to.

```
[csadmin@ContosoLinMT1 ~]$
[csadmin@ContosoLinMT1 ~]$ tar –xvzf Microsoft-ASR_UA_8.2.0.0_RHEL6-64_            .tar.gz
```

If you extracted the installer files to a different directory change directory to the directory to which the contents of the tar archive were extracted. From this directory path execute "sudo ./install.sh"

```
[csadmin@ContosoLinMT1 ~]$ sudo ./install

We trust you have received the usual lecture from the local System
Administrator. It usually boils down to these three things:

    #1) Respect the privacy of others.
    #2) Think before you type.
    #3) With great power comes great responsibility.

[sudo] password for csadmin:

Where do you want to install the agent (default /usr/local/ASR) :

Generating the certificate.

The chosen configuration for this VX is host based configuration...
Checking OS compatibility before installation...

Checking whether RPM package is present...
RPM architecture found is x86_64.


    What is the Primary Role of this Agent ?

    1. Mobility Service

        Select 'Mobility Service' for installation on servers that need to be protected, or
        for servers that act as targets in a failover/failback situation.

    2. Master Target

        Select 'Master Target' for installation on a hypervisor virtual machine that acts
        as the protection target for other protected physical or virtual servers.

Please make your choice ? (1/2) [Default: 1] 2
Configuring Master Target. It takes at least 15 minutes.
```

6. When prompted to make choice of Primary Role of this Agent select 2 (Master Target)

7. Leave the other interactve install options at their default values.

8. Wait for the rest of the installation to proceed and the Host Config Interface to appear. The Host Configuration utility for the Linux Master Target Server is a command line utility. Don't resize your ssh client utility window. Use the arrow keys to select the Global option and press enter on your keyboard.

```
lqqqqqqqqqqqqqqqqqqqqqqqqqqqqqqqqqqqqqqqqqk
x        Host Config Interface          x
xPick the command you wish to run.      x
x          Press ? for help.            x
tqqqqqqqqqqqqqqqqqqqqqqqqqqqqqqqqqqqqqqqqqu
x    Global Agent NAT Logging Quit       x
mqqqqqqqqqqqqqqqqqqqqqqqqqqqqqqqqqqqqqqqqqj
```

```
lqqqqqqqqqqqqqqqqqqqqqqqqqqqqqqqqqqqqk
x          Host Config Interface        x
xPick the command you wish to run.     x
x           Press ? for help.          x
tqqqqqqqqqqqqqqqqqqqqqqqqqqqqqqqqqqqqqu
x   Global Agent NAT Logging Quit      x
mqqqqqqqqqqqqqqqqqqqqqqqqqqqqqqqqqqqqqj
CX Server settings
lqqqqqqqqqqqqqqqqqqqqqqqqk
x     Enter IP Address      x
xIP: 104.40.91.228_____  x
mqqqqqqqqqqqqqqqqqqqqqqqqqj
lqqqqqqqqqqqqqqqqqk
xEnter Port numberx
xPort: 58073_____ x
mqqqqqqqqqqqqqqqqqj
lqqqqqqqqqqqk
xUse https: x
xYes        x
mqqqqqqqqqqqj
lqqqqqqqqqqqqqqqqqqqqqqqqqqqqqqqqqqqk
x            Enter Passphrase         x
xPassphrase: _____ x
mqqqqqqqqqqqqqqqqqqqqqqqqqqqqqqqqqqqqj
```

9. Against the field IP enter the Internal IP address of the Configuration Server obtained from the virtual machines dashboard page and press enter.

10. Against the field Port enter 22 and press enter.

11. Leave Use https: as Yes. Press enter one more time.

12. Enter the Passphrase that was generated on the Configuration Server. If you are using PuTTY client from a Windows machine to ssh to the Linux Master Target Server virtual machine you can use Shift+Insert to paste the contents of the clipboard. Copy the Passphrase to the local clipboard using Ctrl-C and use Shift+Insert to paste it. Press enter

13. Use the right arrow key to navigate to quit and press enter.

14. Wait for the installation to complete

If for some reason you failed to register your Linux Master Target Server to the Configuration Server you could do so again by running the host configuration utility from /usr/local/ASR/Vx/bin/hostconfigcli (you will first need to set access permissions to this directory by executing chmod as a super user)

Validate Master Target Server registration to the Configuration Server.

You can validate that the Master Target Server registered successfully with the Configuration Server by visiting the Server Details page under the Configuration Server page on the Azure Site Recovery vault

Note: After registering the Mt, you might find that the MT is having configuration error with the possible causes - Virtual machine might be deleted from Azure or endpoints are not properly configured. This is because MT configuration is detected by the Azure Endpoints when the MT is deployed in Azure. However this does not hold true for on-premises MT and the error can be ignored. Failback will not have any issues due to this.

Begin protecting the virtual machines back to on-premises

Before failback of the VMs back to on-premises, first you need to protect the virtual machines back to on-premises. Follow the below steps to protect VMs of an application.

Note on temp drive

When a VM is failed over to Azure, it adds an extra temp drive for page file. This is an extra drive that is typically not required by your failed over VM since it might already have a drive dedicated for the page file.

Before you begin reverse protection of the virtual machines, you need to ensure that the drive is taken offline so that it does not get protected.

To do this,

1. Open Computer Management (via control panel administrative tool, or by right click on This PC in the explorer window and selecting manage.)

2. Select Storage Management so that it lists the disks online and attached to the machine.

3. Select the temporary disk attached to the machine and choose to bring it offline.

4. Once it has been successfully taken offline you can proceed with protecting the virtual machine in the reverse direction.

Protection plan for VMs

On the Azure portal, look at the states of the virtual machine and ensure that they are failed over.

NAME		ACTIVE LOCATION	HEALTH	STATUS	REPLICATION STATUS	RPO
Sales-Applications	→	Microsoft Azure	✔ Ok	Unplanned failover completed	✔ Ok	14.95 minutes
Sales-IIS-frontend		Microsoft Azure	✔ Ok	Unplanned failover completed	✔ Ok	24.47 minutes

Note : during failover from Azure back to on-premises, the Azure VM is considered similar to a Physical VM. The failover to on-premises is to a virtual machine.

1. Launch the vContinuum on your machine

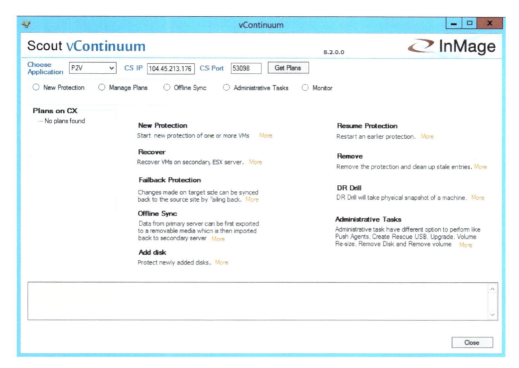

2. In the **Choose Application** setting, select **P2V**

3. Click on the **New Protection** option to begin

4. In the new window that opens you will begin protecting the virtual machines back to on-premises.

-   Select the **OS type** according to the VMs you want to failback and **Get Details**

-   In the **Primary server details**, you need to identify the virtual machines that you want to protect.

-   The virtual machines are listed by their Computer Hostnames and not as they are visible on vCenter or Azure

-   The virtual machines are listed under the vCenter Hostname that the virtual machines were on, before failover.

-   Once you have identified the VMs you want to protect, select them one by one.

5. When you select a virtual machine to protect (and it has already failed over to Azure) you will get a popup window that gives two entries for the virtual machine. This is because the CS has detected two instances of the virtual machines registered to it. You need to remove the entry for the on-premises VM so that you can protect the correct VM. Note that you will see the entries by its computer hostname. To identify the correct Azure VM entry here, you

can log into the Azure VM and go to C:\Program Files (x86)\Microsoft Azure Site Recovery\Application Data\etc. In the file drscout.conf , identify the Host ID. In the vContinuum dialog, keep the entry for which the hostID is found in the VM. Delete all other entries.

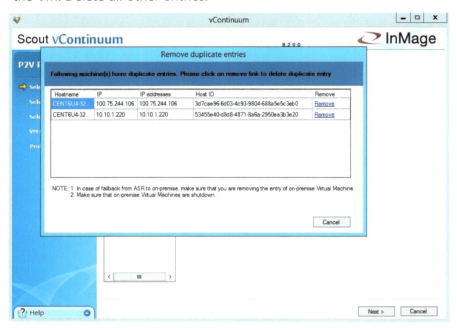

6. To select the correct VM you can refer to its IP address. The IP address range on-premises will be the on-premises VM.

7. Click **Remove** to delete the entry.

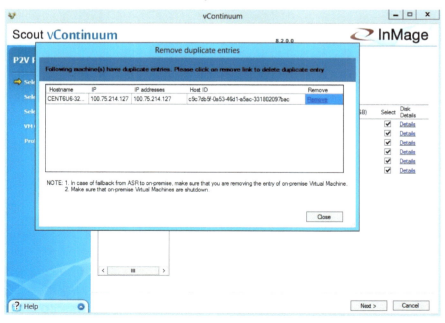

8. Go to the vCenter and stop the virtual machine on the vCenter

9. Next you can also delete the virtual machines on-premises

1. Next you need to specify the on-premises MT server to which you want to protect the VMs.

2. To do this, connect to the vCenter to which you want to failback to

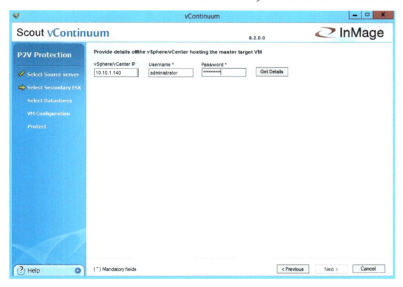

3. Select the MT server based on the host into which you want to recover the virtual machines

1. Next provide the replication option for each of the virtual machines

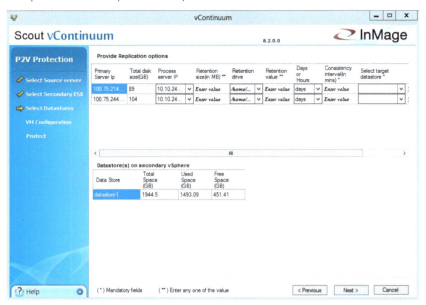

2. To do this you need to select the recovery side **Datastore** – this is the datastore to which the VMs will be recovered to.

The different options you need to provide per VM are

OPTION	OPTION RECOMMENDED VALUE
Process Server IP	Select the PS which you have deployed on Azure
Retention size in MB	
Retention value	1
Days/Hours	Days
Consistency	1

OPTION	OPTION RECOMMENDED VALUE
Interval	
Select Target Datastore	The datastore available on the recovery side. This data store should have enough space and also be available to the ESX host on which you want to realise the virtual machine.

3. Next you can configure the properties that the virtual machine will acquire after failover to on-premises site. The different properties you can configure are as below

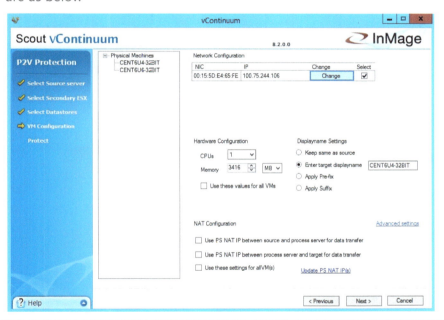

PROPERTY	HOW TO CONFIGURE
Network Configuration	For each NIC detected, configure the failback IP address for the virtual machine. Select the NIC and click **Change** to specify the IP address details.
Hardware	You can specify the CPU and the Memory values for the VM. This

PROPERTY	HOW TO CONFIGURE
Configuration	setting can be applied to all the VMs you are trying to protect.
Display Name	To identify the correct values for the CPU and Memory, you can refer to the IAAS VMs role size and see the number of cores and Memory assigned.
Display Name	After failover back to on-premises, you can choose to rename the virtual machines as it will be seen in the inventory of vCenter. Note that the default value seen here is the virtual machine computer host name. To identify the VM name, you can refer to the VM list in the Protection group.
NAT Configuration	Discussed in detail below

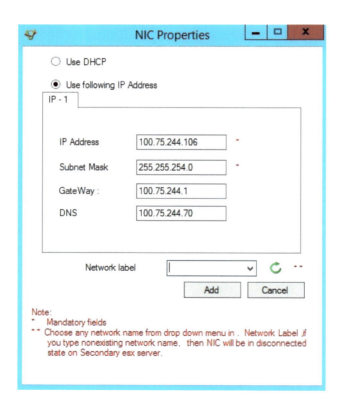

PS NAT settings choices

To enable protection of the virtual machines, two communication channels need to be established.

The first channel is between the virtual machine and the Process Server. This channel collects the data from the VM and sends it to the PS. PS will then send this data to the Master Target. If the process server and the virtual machine to be protected are on the same Azure vNet, then you do not need to use the NAT settings. If the PS and the virtual machine to be protected is in two different vNet, then you need to specify the NAT settings for the PS and check the first option.

☐ Use PS NAT IP between source and process server for data transfer

To identify the Process server Public IP, you can go to the PS deployment in Azure and see its Public IP address.

The second channel is between the Process server and the Master target. The option to use NAT or not depends on whether you are using VPN based connection between MT and PS or protecting over the internet. If the PS communicates to the MT over a VPN, then you should not select this option. If the Master Target needs to communicate to the Process server over the internet, then specify the NAT settings for the PS.

☐ Use PS NAT IP between process server and target for data transfer

To identify the Process server Public IP, you can go to the PS deployment in Azure and see its Public IP address.

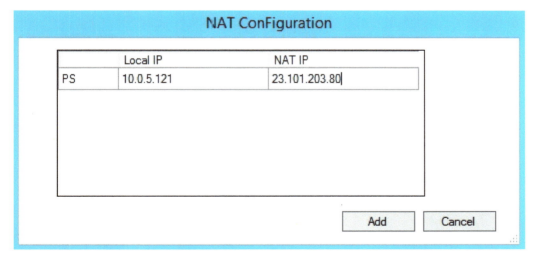

1. If you have not deleted the on-premises virtual machines as specified in Step 5.d, and if the datastore you are failing back to, as selected in step 7.a still contains the old VMDK's then you will also need to ensure that the failback VM gets created in a new place. For this you can select the Advanced settings

and specify an alternate Folder to restore to in the **Folder Name Settings** section of the Advanced Settings.

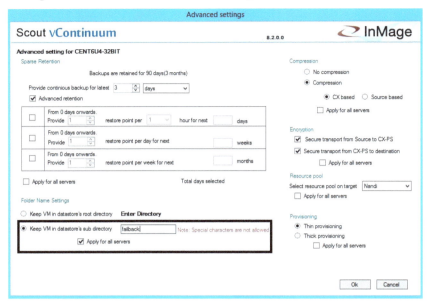

The other options in the Advanced settings can be left as default. Make sure you apply the folder name settings to all the servers.

2. Next move to the final stage of the Protection. Here you need to run a Readiness Check to ensure that the virtual machines are ready to be protected back to on-premises.

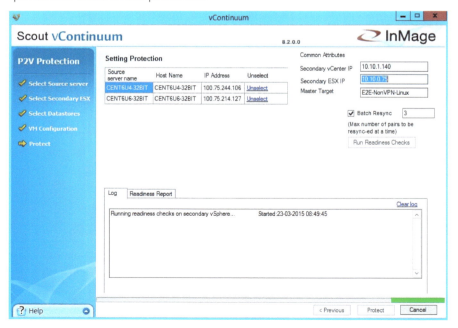

Copy

a. Click on the readiness check and wait for it to complete.

b. The Readiness Report tab will give the information if all the virtual machines are ready.

c. If the Readiness Report is successful on all the virtual machines it will allow you to specify a name to the Protection plan

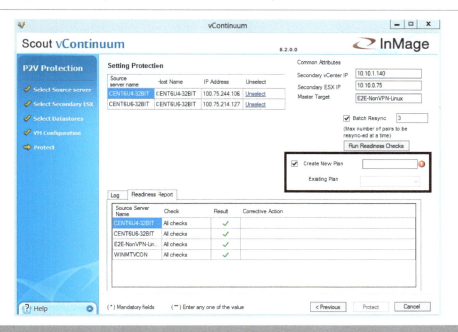

Copy

d. Give the plan a new Name and begin Protect by clicking the button below.

3. The Protection will now begin.

  • You can see the progress of the protection on the vContinuum

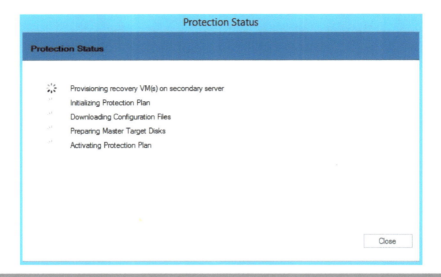

Copy

b. Once the step **Activating Protection Plan** is completed, you can monitor the protection of the virtual machines via the ASR Portal.

c. You can also monitor the protection via Azure Site Recovery.

You can also see the exact status of the pairs by clicking into the virtual machine and monitoring its progress under the volume replication section.

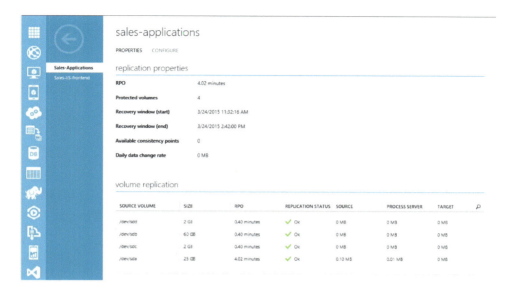

Prepare the Failback Plan

You can prepare a failback plan using vContinuum so that the application can be failed over back to on-premises at any time. These recovery plans are very similar to the ASR Recovery plans.

1. Launch the vContinuum and select the option to **Manage plans**.

2. User the sub-options select **Recover.**

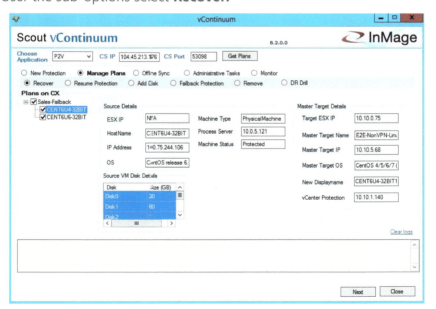

3. You can see the list of all the Plans that have been used to protect the virtual machines. These are the same plans you can use to recover.

4. Select the Protection Plan and select all the VMs you want to recover within it.

5. On selecting each VM you can see more details about the source VM, target ESX server where the VM will be recovered to and the source VM disk

6. Click Next to begin the **Recover** Wizard

7. Select the Virtual Machines you want to recover

See the list of all the virtual machines that you can recover

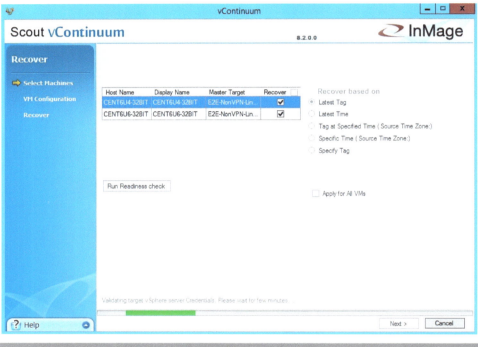

Copy

b. You can **recover based on** multiple options however we recommend the **Latest Tag.** This will ensure that the latest data from the virtual machine will be used.

c. Select **Apply for All VMs** to ensure that the latest tag will be chosen for all the virtual machines.

8. Run the **Readiness Check.** This will inform if the right parameters are configured to enable the latest tag recovery of the virtual machine. Click Next if all the checks are successful else look at the log and resolve the errors.

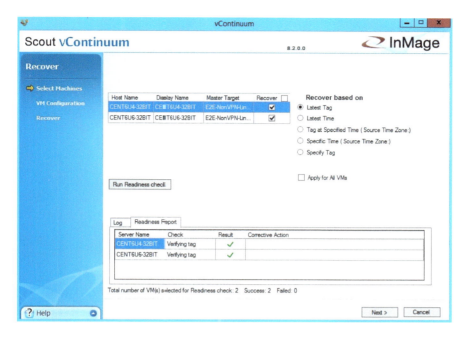

9. In the VM Configuration step of the wizard, ensure that the recovery settings are correctly set. In case the VM settings are different from the one you require, you can choose to change them. Since we have already completed this action during the protection, you may choose to ignore it this time.

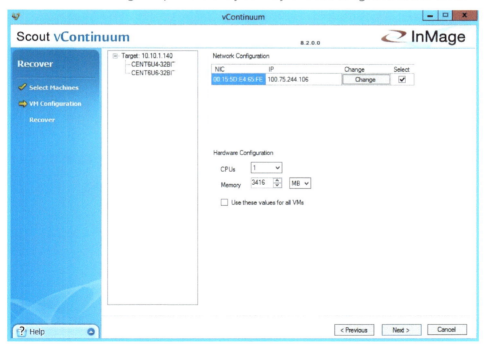

10. Finally review the list of virtual machines that will be recovered.

- Specify a recovery order to the virtual machines.

Note: The virtual machines are listed using the Computer Hostname. It might be difficult to map the computer hostname to the virtual machine. To map the names, you can go to the virtual machines dashboard in Azure IAAS and look at the hostname of the virtual machine.

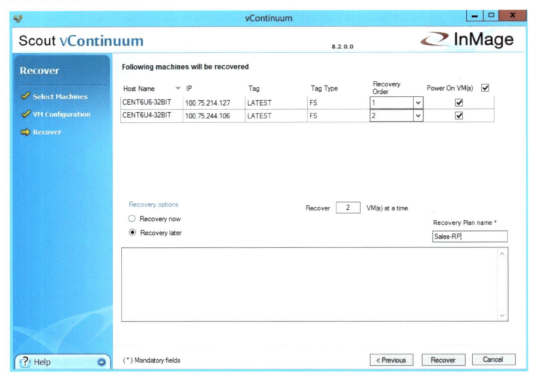

1. Give the **recovery plan name** and select **Recover later** in **Recovery options.**

   - In case you want to recover right away you can choose to **Recover now** in the **Recovery options**.

   - It is recommended to Recover later since the protection initial replication may not have completed

   - Finally click on **Recover** button to either save the plan or to trigger the recovery based on your **Recovery options**.

2. You can see the Recovery Status and see if it the plan is successfully saved.

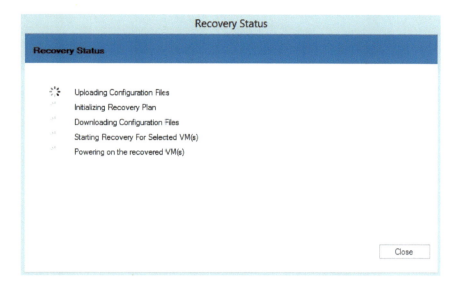

3. If you have chosen to recover later, you will be informed that the plan is created and you can recover later.

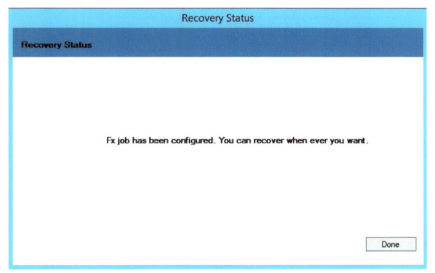

Recover Virtual Machines

After the plan is created, you can choose to recover the virtual machines. As a pre-requisite, you need to ensure that the virtual machines have completed synchronization.

sales-pg

VIRTUAL MACHINES   CONFIGURE

NAME	↑	ACTIVE LOCATION	HEALTH	STATUS	REPLICATION STATUS	RPO
Sales-Applications	→	Microsoft Azure	✔ Ok	Unplanned failover completed	✔ Ok	8.67 minutes
Sales-IIS-frontend		Microsoft Azure	✔ Ok	Unplanned failover completed	✔ Ok	4.40 minutes

If Replication Status shows OK then the protection is completed and the RPO threshold has been met. To confirm the replication pair's health, you can go to the virtual machine properties and see the health of the replication.

Turn off the Azure virtual machines before you initiate the recovery. This will ensure that there is no split brain and your end customers will be served by one copy of the application. Only when you have successfully ensured that the Azure VMs are turned off continue to the steps below.

To begin recovering the virtual machines back to on-premise, you need to start the plan that is saved.

1. On the vContinuum select to **Monitor** the plans.

2. The wizard will list the plans that have been executed till now.

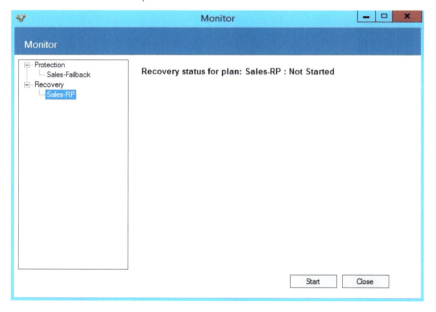

3. Select the **Recovery** node and select the plan that you want to recover.

   - It will inform you that the plan has not yet started.

4. Click **Start** to begin the recovery.

5. You can monitor the recovery of the virtual machines

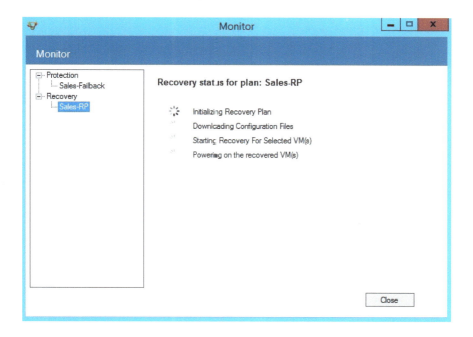

6. Once the VMs have been powered ON, you can connect to the virtual machines on your vCenter.
   Re-protect to Azure after failback

After failback has been completed you may want to protect the virtual machines once again. The below steps will help you re-configure the protection

1. Check that the virtual machines on-premises are working and application is able to reach your end customers.

2. On the Azure Site Recovery portal, select the virtual machines and delete them. Select to disable the protection of the virtual machines. This will ensure that the VMs are no more protected.

3. Go to the Azure IAAS virtual machines and delete the failed over VMs.

4. Delete the old VMs on vSpehere – these are the VMs that you previously failed over to Azure.

5. On the ASR portal select to protect the virtual machines recently failed over.

6. Once the VMs are protected, you can add them to a recovery plan and be continuously protected.

Manage your process servers

The process server sends replication data to the master target server in Azure, and discovers new VMware virtual machines added to a vCenter server. In the following circumstances you might want to change the process server in your deployment:

- If the current process server goes down

- If your recovery point objective (RPO) rises to an unacceptable level for your organization.

If required you can move the replication of some or all of your on-premises VMware virtual machines and physical servers to a different process server. For example:

- **Failure**—If a process server fails or isn't available you can move protected machine replication to another process server. Metadata of the source machine and replica machine will be moved to the new process server and data is resynchronized. The new process server will automatically connect to the vCenter server to perform automatic discovery. You can monitor the state of process servers on the Site Recovery dashboard.

- **Load balancing to adjust RPO**—For improved load balancing you can select a different process server in the Site Recovery portal, and move replication of one or more machines to it for manual load balancing. In this case metadata of the selected source and replica machines is moved to the new process server. The original process server remains connected to the vCenter server.

Monitor the process server

If a process server is in a critical state a status warning will be displayed on the Site Recovery Dashboard. You can click on the status to open the Events tab and then drill down to specific jobs on the Jobs tab.

Modify the process server used for replication

1. Go to the **CONFIGURATION SERVERS** page under **SERVERS**

2. Click on the name of the Configuration Server and go to **Server Details**.

3. In the **Process Servers** list click **Change Process Server** next to the server you want to modify.

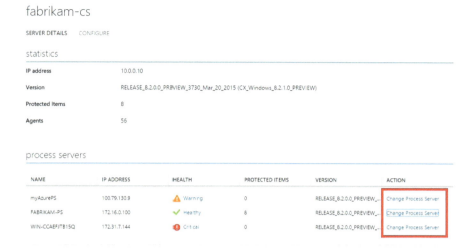

4. In the **Change Process Server** dialog select the new server in **Target Process Server**, and then select the virtual machines that you want to replicate to the new server. click the information icon next to the server name to get information about it, including free space, used memory. The average space that will be required to replicate each selected virtual machine to the new process server is displayed to help you make load decisions.

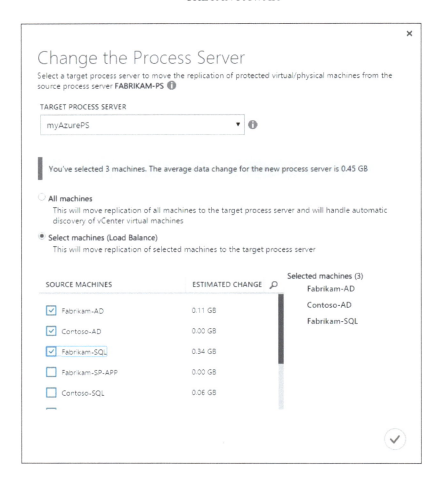

5. Click the check mark to begin replicating to the new process server. If you remove all virtual machines from a process server that was critical it should no longer display a critical warning in the dashboard.

Different ASR Scenarios

Replicate between an on-premises physical server or VMware virtual machine and Azure

If you want to protect either VMware VMs, or Windows/Linux physical machines by replicating them to Azure here's what you'll need.

LOCATION   WHAT YOU NEED

LOCATION	WHAT YOU NEED
On-premises	**Process server**: This server optimizes data from protected VMware virtual machines or physical Windows/Linux machines before sending it to Azure. It also handles push installation of the Mobility service component to protected machine, and performs automatic discovery of VMware virtual machines.
	VMware vCenter server: If you're protecting VMware VMs you'll need a VMwave vCenter server managing your vSphere hypervisors
	ESX server: If you're protecting VMware VMs you'll need a server running ESX/ESX version 5.1 or 5.5 with the latest updates.
	Machines: If you're protecting VMware you should have VMware VMs with VMware tools installed and running. If you're protecting physical machines they should be running a supported Windows or Linux operating system. See what's supported.
	Mobility service: Installs on machines you want to protect to capture changes and communicate them to the process server.
	Third-party components: This deployment depends on some third-party components.
Azure	**Configuration server**: Standard A3 Azure VM that coordinates communication between protected machines, the process server, and master target servers in Azure. It sets up replication and coordinates recovery when failover occurs.
	Master target server: Azure VM that holds replicated data from protected machines using attached VHDs created on blob storage in your Azure storage account. A failback master target server runs on premises so that you can fail back Azure VMs to VMware VMs.
	Site Recovery vault: At least one Azure Site Recovery vault (set up

LOCATION	WHAT YOU NEED
	with a subscription to the Site Recovery service)
	Virtual network: An Azure network on which the configuration server and master target servers are located, in the same subscription and region as the Site Recovery service.
	Azure storage: Azure storage account to store replicated data. Should be a standard geo-redundant or premium account in the same region as the Site Recovery subscription.

In this scenario communications can occur over a a VPN connection to internal ports on the Azure network (using Azure ExpressRoute or a site-to-site VPN), or over a secure internet connection to the mapped public endpoints on the Azure cloud service for the configuration and master target server VMs.

The Mobility service on protected machines sends replication data the process server, and sends replication metadata to the configuration server. The process server communicates with configuration server for management and control information. It sends replication information to the master target server and it optimizes and sends replicated data to the master target server.

Replicating Hyper-V VMs to Azure (with VMM)

If you're VMs are located on a Hyper-V host that's managed in a System Center VMM cloud here's what you'll need in order to replicate them to Azure.

LOCATION	WHAT YOU NEED
On-premises	**VMM server**: At least one VMM server set up with at least one VMM private cloud. The Azure Site Recovery Provider will be installed on each VMM server
	Hyper-V server: At least one Hyper-V host server located in the VMM cloud. The Microsoft Recovery Services agent will be installed on each Hyper-V server.

LOCATION	WHAT YOU NEED
	Virtual machines: At least one virtual machine running on the Hyper-V server. Nothing gets installed on the virtual machine.
Azure	**Site Recovery vault**: At least one Azure Site Recovery vault (set up with a subscription to the Site Recovery service)
	Storage account: An Azure storage account under the same subscription as the Site Recovery service. Replicated machines are stored in Azure storage.

In this scenario the Provider running on the VMM server coordinates and orchestrates replication with the Site Recovery service over the internet. Data is replicated between the Recovery Services agent running on the on-premises Hyper-V server and Azure storage over HTTPS 443. Communications from both the Provider and the agent are secure and encrypted. Replicated data in Azure storage is also encrypted.

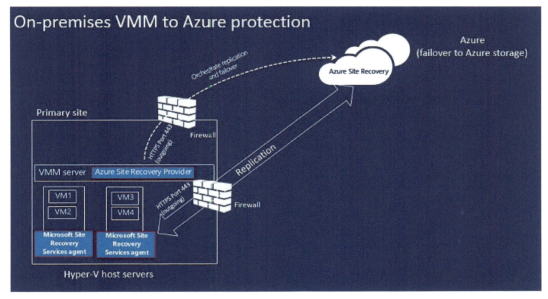

Replicating Hyper-V VMs to Azure (without VMM)

If your VMs aren't managed by a System Center VMM server here's what you'll need to do to replicate them to Azure

LOCATION	WHAT YOU NEED
On-premises	**Hyper-V server**: At least one Hyper-V host server. The Azure Site Recovery Provider and the Microsoft Recovery Services agent will be installed on each Hyper-V server.
	Virtual machines: At least one virtual machine running on the Hyper-V server. Nothing gets installed on the virtual machine.
Azure	**Site Recovery vault**: At least one Azure Site Recovery vault (set up with a subscription to the Site Recovery service)
	Storage account: An Azure storage account under the same subscription as the Site Recovery service. Replicated machines are stored in Azure storage.

In this scenario the Provider running on the Hyper-V server coordinates and orchestrates replication with the Site Recovery service over the internet. Data is replicated between the Recovery Services agent running on the on-premises Hyper-V server and Azure storage over HTTPS 443. Communications from both the Provider and the agent are secure and encrypted. Replicated data in Azure storage is also encrypted.

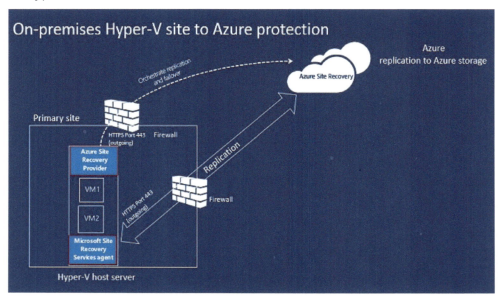

Replicate Hyper-V VMs to a secondary datacenter

If you want to protect your Hyper-V VMs by replicating them to a secondary datacenter here's what you'll need to do. Note that you can only do this if your Hyper-V host server is managed in a System Center VMM cloud.

LOCATION	WHAT YOU NEED
On-premises	**VMM server**: A VMM server in the primary site and one in the secondary site The Azure Site Recovery Provider will be installed on each VMM server.
	Hyper-V server: At least one Hyper-V host server located in a VMM cloud in the primary and secondary sites. Nothing gets installed on the Hyper-V servers
	Virtual machines: At least one virtual machine running on the Hyper-V server. Nothing gets installed on the virtual machine.
Azure	**Site Recovery vault**: At least one Azure Site Recovery vault (set up with a subscription to the Site Recovery service).

In this scenario the Provider on the VMM server coordinates and orchestrates replication with the Site Recovery service over the internet. Data is replicated between the primary and secondary Hyper-V host servers over the internet using Kerberos or certificate authentication. Communications from both the Provider and between Hyper-V host servers are secure and encrypted.

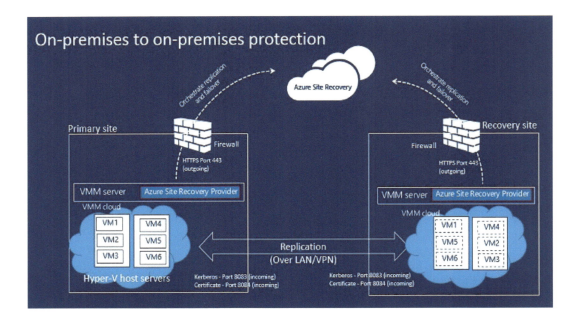

Replicate Hyper-V VMs to a secondary datacenter with SAN replication

If your VMs are located on a Hyper-V host that's managed in a System Center VMM cloud and you're using SAN storage here's what you'll need in order to replicate between two datacenters.

LOCATION	WHAT YOU NEED
Primary datacenter	**SAN array**: A supported SAN array managed by the primary VMM server. The SAN shares a network infrastructure with another SAN array in the secondary site
	VMM server: At least one VMM server with one or more VMM clouds and replication groups set up. The Azure Site Recovery Provider will be installed on each VMM server.
	Hyper-V server: At least one Hyper-V host server with virtual machines, located in a replication group. Nothing gets installed on the Hyper-V host servers.
	Virtual machines: At least one virtual machine running on the Hyper-V host server. Nothing gets installed on the virtual machine.

LOCATION	WHAT YOU NEED
Secondary datacenter	**SAN array**: A supported SAN array managed by the secondary VMM server. **VMM server**: At least one VMM server with one or more VMM clouds. **Hyper-V server**: At least one Hyper-V host server.
Azure	**Site Recovery vault**: At least one Azure Site Recovery vault (set up with a subscription to the Site Recovery service)

In this scenario the Provider on the VMM server coordinates and orchestrates replication with the Site Recovery service over the internet. Data is replicated between the primary and secondary storage arrays using synchronous SAN replication.

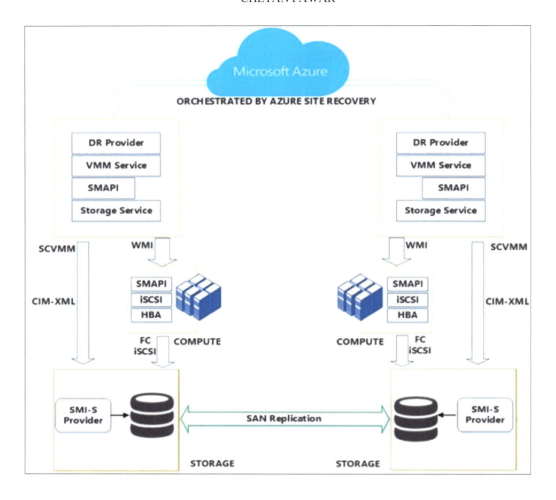

Replicate VMware virtual machines and physical servers to Azure

You can replicate VMware virtual machines and physical servers (Windows/Linux) to Azure over a VPN site-to-site connection or over the internet.

Replicate over a VPN site-to-site connection (or ExpressRoute) to Azure

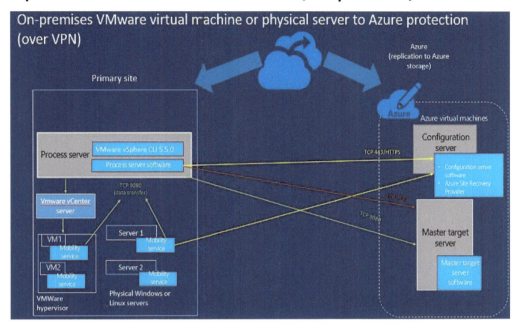

Replicate over the internet

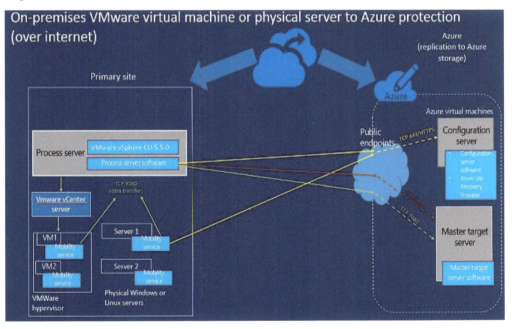

Replicate between on-premises physical servers or VMware virtual machines in primary and secondary datacenters

If you want to protect either VMware VMs, or Windows/Linux physical machines by replicating them between two on-premises datacenters here's what you'll need.

LOCATION	WHAT YOU NEED
On-premises primary	**Process server**: Set up the process server component in your primary site to handle caching, compression, and data optimization. It also handles push installation of the Unified Agent to machines you want to protect. **VMware protection**: If you're protecting VMware VMs you'll need a VMware EXS/ESXi hypervisor or a VMware vCenter server managing multiple hypervisors **Physical server protection**: If you're protecting physical machines they should be running Windows or Linux. **Unified Agent**: Installs on machines you want to protect and on the machine that operates as the master target server. It acts as a communication provider between all the InMage components.
On-premises secondary	**Configuration server**: The configuration server is the first component you install, and it's installed on the secondary site to manage, configure, and monitor your deployment, either using the management website or the vContinuum console. The configuration server also includes the push mechanism for remote deployment of the Unified Agent. There's only a single configuration server in a deployment and it must be installed on a machine running Windows Server 2012 R2. **vContinuum server**: Install in the same location (secondary site) as the configuration server. It provides a console for managing and monitoring your protected environment. In a default install the

LOCATION	WHAT YOU NEED
	vContinuum server is the first master target server and has the Unified Agent installed. **Master target server**: The master target server holds replicated data. It receives data from the process server and creates a replica machine in the secondary site, and holds the data retention points. The number of master target servers you need depends on the number of machines you're protecting. If you want to fail back to the primary site you'll need a master target server there too.
Azure	**Site Recovery vault**: At least one Azure Site Recovery vault (set up with a subscript on to the Site Recovery service). You download InMage Scout to set up the deployment after creating the vault. You also install the latest update for all the InMage component servers.

In this scenario delta replication changes are sent from the Unified Agent running on the protected machine to the process server. The process server optimizes this data and transfers it to the master target server on the secondary site. The configuration server manages the replication process.

www.ingramcontent.com/pod-product-compliance
Lightning Source LLC
Chambersburg PA
CBHW041419050326
40689CB00002B/577